PRODUCTIVE PERFORMANCE APPRAISALS

SECOND EDITION

PRODUCTIVE PERFORMANCE APPRAISALS

SECOND EDITION

Paul Falcone
with Randi Sachs

AMACOM
AMERICAN MANAGEMENT ASSOCIATION
New York • Atlanta • Brussels • Chicago • Mexico City • San Francisco
Shanghai • Tokyo • Toronto • Washington, D.C.

Special discounts on bulk quantities of AMACOM books are available to corporations, professional associations, and other organizations. For details, contact Special Sales Department, AMACOM, a division of American Management Association, 1601 Broadway, New York, NY 10019.
Tel: 212-903-8316. Fax: 212-903-8083.
E-mail: specialsls@amanet.org
Website: www.amacombooks.org/go/specialsales
To view all AMACOM titles go to: www.amacombooks.org

This publication is designed to provide accurate and authoritative information in regard to the subject matter covered. It is sold with the understanding that the publisher is not engaged in rendering legal, accounting, or other professional service. If legal advice or other expert assistance is required, the services of a competent professional person should be sought.

Library of Congress Cataloging-in-Publication Data

Falcone, Paul.
        Productive performance appraisals / Paul Falcone, with Randi Sachs.—2nd ed.
            p.   cm. — (WorkSmart)
        Previous ed. was entered under Randi Sachs.
        Includes index.
        ISBN-10: 0-8144-7422-5 (pbk.)
        ISBN-13: 978-0-8144-7422-8 (pbk.)
        1. Employees—Rating of.   I. Sachs, Randi Toler.   II. Sachs, Randi Toler.
        Productive performance appraisals.   III. Title.

        HF5549.5.R3F37   2007
        658.3'125—dc22   2006036462

Printing number

10   9   8   7   6   5   4   3   2   1

CONTENTS

Preface   vii

PART I

THE PRODUCTIVE APPRAISAL

Chapter 1	What's the Point?	3
Chapter 2	It's as Easy as One, Two, Three	10
Chapter 3	Face-to-Face	18

PART II

HOW TO MAKE IT HAPPEN: ADVANCE PREPARATIONS

Chapter 4	Plan for the Future	33
Chapter 5	Document, Document, Document	43
Chapter 6	Prepare Yourself	54
Chapter 7	Prepare Your Employee	62

PART III

COMMON PROBLEMS AND EFFECTIVE SOLUTIONS

Chapter 8	When You Disagree on Roles and Goals	69
Chapter 9	When the News Is Bad	78
Chapter 10	Watch Out for Pitfalls	87

PART IV

WRAPPING IT UP

Chapter 11	The Post-Appraisal Meeting	95
Chapter 12	You're Ready to Go	104
Index		111
About the Authors		115

PREFACE

Does the thought of conducting performance appraisals for your employees make you cringe? Is it something you tend to put off until you "have the time"? Does the idea of telling grown men and women that they have not been "living up to their potential" make your palms sweat and your throat dry? Don't feel bad. You are not alone.

Many supervisors look upon performance appraisals as one of the most uncomfortable tasks that they are called upon to do, and if they had a say in it, they might eliminate altogether any formal meeting that could be called a performance appraisal. But their feelings—and possibly yours—are a bit out of focus. Performance appraisals serve a very useful role in the workplace and, if done right, provide you with an exceptionally powerful management tool. And believe it or not, the process need not be unpleasant for you.

It is not unusual for someone who rose from the ranks or is right out of initial management training to find it uncomfortable to "get personal" and evaluate another person's performance—especially face-to-face! The review of one employee or another will give you trouble for any number of reasons: The employee may be a discipline problem; she may be very sensitive; he may have nowhere to go within your organization. . . . There are as many possible reasons as there are employees.

Just keep in mind, however, that more and more CEOs are looking to their frontline managers and human resources departments to maximize their return on investment (ROI) of human capital. That may sound like a fancy term, but in a knowledge-based economy, a company's "human assets" often serve as that organization's primary profit lever. Simply stated, a company that has the strongest and most creative human capital assets (i.e., employees) often wins at the game of business.

If CEOs and CFOs are focusing more on measuring the ROI of human capital, then those *quantitative* metrics that drive organizational performance must somehow be supported by or linked to some sort of *qualitative* foundation. That qualitative foundation can best be found in each individual worker's performance appraisal. In short, that's where the rubber meets the road, and it represents the kernel of measurement of individual performance that rolls up into the company's overall productivity results.

This book will help you overcome your fear of conducting performance appraisals by giving you straightforward advice on:

- How to prepare for each employee's interview
- How to structure a performance appraisal
- How to put yourself and your employees at ease
- How to make the performance appraisal a collaborative effort between you and your employees
- How to strengthen your relationship with your employees by conducting productive reviews
- How to handle employees who have performance or conduct problems

In addition, you will realize that the "performance appraisal," per se, isn't as much a form as it is a process—a means rather than an end. It is a system of ongoing feedback; recognition; and, when necessary, redirection that helps you, the supervisor, lead effectively and stand out as a rarity among your peers. It also represents a system of ongoing engagement with your subordinates that creates for them an environment of job satisfaction and motivation (which, of course, typically results in greater retention). Most important, it is a process that will help you build a culture that focuses on performance excellence.

On a more personal note, by investing time in mastering this critical management tool and system, you will also gain portable, sought-after skills that, over the course of your career, will help you delegate more effectively (i.e., work easier), make more money, and advance more rapidly. Now let's read on so that you can learn to develop your own style for giving performance appraisals and leading and motivating your staff.

PRODUCTIVE PERFORMANCE APPRAISALS

SECOND EDITION

PART I

1

THE PRODUCTIVE APPRAISAL

CHAPTER 1

WHAT'S THE POINT?

"You wanted to see me, Ed?"

"Yes, Dan, come right in. As you know, it's been one year since your last performance appraisal. I want you to know that I've been very pleased with your work. I feel I can really count on you when I need something done right."

"Thanks, Ed. That's nice to hear."

"Tell me, how has everything been going on your end? Is there anything you would like to talk about? I've got some time now, for a change."

"Gee, I can't think of anything right now. Except that . . ."

"What is it, Dan?"

"Well, ever since they moved the coffee machine near my work-station, I've been bothered by all the noise and conversation that seem to go along with the coffee."

"We'll just move it then. I don't want one of my top workers distracted like that. Just give me a few days, okay?"

"Sure, Ed. Thanks."

"Well, we'll need to put together an annual review for you, so I'll get to work on it right away. Keep up the good work, Dan, and

3

I'll do my best to get you whatever's in the merit pool this year. There should be nothing to worry about."

"Okay, Ed. Thanks for the good words."

"You're very welcome. And thank *you*. You make my job that much easier."

Ed, the supervisor in the preceding scenario, is probably feeling very happy with himself. He can check that performance appraisal off his "to do" list now. He believes that he has fulfilled his obligations by telling his employee that he has been doing a great job and to "keep up the good work."

"These types of performance appraisals are simple," Ed says to himself. *"I have no complaints, and money is not an issue. These types of appraisals are short and sweet. Now I can get back to work."*

Poor Ed is under an all-too-common delusion that performance appraisals are used either to give good employees a pat on the back or to put the pressure on unsatisfactory employees to improve their performance. What Ed doesn't know is that performance appraisals require advance preparation and that the meeting itself can and should be a collaborative planning session during which both supervisor and employee can take an in-depth look at past and current performances and can together make plans for the future.

Whether your employee is a good worker or a thorn in your side, you can make your performance appraisals productive sessions that will benefit you both.

By reading this book you've taken the first step in deciding to make the performance appraisal process truly worthwhile. For many of us, reviewing the work of others is one of the more difficult aspects of being a supervisor. You may not feel fully qualified to play judge and jury over every employee. However, if you follow the advice offered here, you can actually eliminate some of the burden of that responsibility. By making the performance appraisal a collaborative effort, you will ultimately share some of the decision making with your employee. More important, you will be able to use your performance appraisals to improve the productivity of your employees and, ultimately, of your entire department.

HOW CAN APPRAISALS BE PRODUCTIVE?

A common misconception is that the sole purpose of an appraisal is to inform employees how their performance has been rated. That's unfortunate, because a productive performance appraisal can accomplish much more (see Figure 1-1). A productive appraisal, along with reviewing the quality of the employee's work, serves as a work session between supervisor and employee in which you take the time and effort to meet with an individual and set new goals and objectives for the coming year. A productive appraisal recognizes that people are an incredibly valuable resource with specific needs and goals.

Recall the discussion between Ed, the supervisor, and Dan, his employee. What do you notice about Dan's part in the conversa-

FIGURE 1-1. BENEFITS OF PRODUCTIVE PERFORMANCE APPRAISALS.

- Employees learn about their own strengths in addition to weaknesses.
- New goals and objectives are agreed upon.
- Employees are active participants in the evaluation process.
- The relationship between supervisor and employees is taken to an adult-to-adult level.
- Work teams may be restructured for maximum efficiency.
- Employees renew their interest in being a part of the organization, now and in the future.
- Training needs are identified.
- Time is devoted to discussing quality of work without regard to money issues.
- The supervisor becomes more comfortable in reviewing the performance of employees.
- Organizational impediments can be identified that hinder the workflow.
- Employees feel that they are "heard" and taken seriously as individuals and that the supervisor is truly concerned about their needs and goals.

tion? If you said, "There wasn't much to it," you're on the right track. Ed really didn't give Dan much of an opportunity to talk. In fact, most of his questions required little more than one-word answers.

One reason you may dread giving performance reviews is that you feel obligated to do most of the talking. You think you must have a prepared speech to give your employee. However, in a productive appraisal, this is not the case. Your appraisal session should not be a one-way monologue. Instead, you should meet with your employee and engage in a true conversation. In addition to giving your own opinions about the employee's past performance and future potential, you should listen carefully to what your employee has to say. Furthermore, you will actually make decisions about future assignments and goals based on what both you and the employee decide *together.*

In Ed's "review" of Dan, not a word was said about preparing new goals for the coming year. Ed's reasoning may have been that because he was not promoting Dan and there were no problems with Dan's performance or productivity, a new goal-setting session would not be necessary. Ed is wrong, of course. Even the best performers should be given new goals to strive for, or else their interest in the job may wane. It's natural for people to want to better themselves, to earn the intrinsic rewards of doing well and improving. Even if job titles or responsibilities do not change appreciably, goals can still be set to improve efficiency and quality of work and new objectives can be identified. Indeed, by neglecting to set new goals, you may be giving the message that if employees want to move ahead they will have to do it at another place of work.

IT'S THE PROCESS THAT COUNTS

"Okay," you say. "I agree that it is important to set new goals for each of my employees periodically, and performance reviews are certainly convenient times to do so. But isn't the supervisor the best judge of what these goals should be? After all, I know the direction that the entire department will be headed in the coming year.

I know where I can best use each of my employees. Wouldn't it be better to present each employee with my own findings and see if we are in agreement?"

The short answer is a succinct no. Here are a few reasons why:

■ When goals are set without input from the employee, there is much less motivation for these goals to be realized.

■ The direction of the department must reflect the interests, abilities, and motivations of the employees who comprise it, or else the supervisor will face a continual, uphill battle to meet these objectives.

■ Presented with a set of objectives predetermined by the supervisor, not only will most employees accept them as what they need to do to meet with full approval from their supervisor, but they will also believe that their abilities are limited to the list of goals they are given.

The most important benefit, however, can be described as the *secret weapon*—what makes it all worthwhile. The most important result of the performance appraisal is not that the employee is given a rating of the quality of her work, it is not that the employee comes away from the meeting with new performance objectives and career goals, and it is not that the employee has been given enough positive feedback to last him for another year (which, by the way, is never the case).

The most important result of the performance appraisal is *the actual process itself.*

By working together to analyze and evaluate the employee's performance as well as his place within the department and the organization as a whole, and by setting goals for the near- and long-term future, you and your employee can strengthen your relationship and become a team of two adults working toward a common, agreed-upon goal.

This is the "psychic" income that people derive from work. It comes from open communication with and recognition from the boss—the two most important factors in retaining key talent, and the two most-often-cited reasons why people leave their companies to pursue opportunities elsewhere. Remember, they say that *people join companies and leave managers*. It's also said that the difference between an active and a passive job seeker is one bad day in the office. Failing to provide your staff with these key motivational drivers may lead to premature turnover and a poor retention record, and that may in turn reflect negatively on *your* next performance review.

In the following chapters you will learn how to revamp the performance appraisals you give your employees. Instead of annual pep talks, they'll be ongoing work sessions that will help each employee continue to grow in her job and will help you renew that employee's commitment to the organization.

Whether you are a novice or an experienced supervisor, you can improve the quality of the reviews that you give and, ultimately, the relationships that you share and the performance results that you achieve. We realize, of course, that many companies have set policies and guidelines that require you to carry out performance appraisals in a certain way. The message in this book can transcend different requirements. Take what you can from this book and adapt it for your own personal use. For a sample of what lessons are to come, take the Do You or Don't You? test that follows to see how many of the recommended techniques you are already using. When you are done, continue reading. You'll find that conducting productive appraisals is not as hard as you may think.

TEST YOURSELF—DO YOU OR DON'T YOU?

Read the following statements regarding performance appraisals and indicate your feelings about them. Check either "I do" or "I don't."

❏ I do   ❏ I don't: keep a performance log on each of my employees and update it frequently.

❏ I do   ❏ I don't: prepare my employees in advance of reviews and ask them to complete a self-evaluation sheet.

❑ I do ❑ I don't: treat monetary issues and promotions separately from performance appraisal discussions.

❑ I do ❑ I don't: get my employees' input before making decisions on reassignments or new tasks.

❑ I do ❑ I don't: hold all performance reviews in a private setting and at a time when we will not be disturbed.

❑ I do ❑ I don't: know how to give employees criticism without arousing hostility.

❑ I do ❑ I don't: know what "not to say" in a performance review.

❑ I do ❑ I don't: feel that giving performance reviews is a good use of my time.

❑ I do ❑ I don't: feel comfortable giving performance appraisals to all of my employees.

❑ I do ❑ I don't: always follow up on areas of concern that come up during appraisal interviews.

❑ I do ❑ I don't: discuss both what the employee has done right and wrong during a performance review.

CHAPTER 2

IT'S AS EASY AS ONE, TWO, THREE

I f you want to get the maximum value out of the performance appraisals you give, you have to put some effort into them. An ideal performance appraisal is actually a three-step affair. Let's go over each individual step first and then discuss why all three are needed to do the job right.

STEP 1: EVALUATION AND JOB ANALYSIS

An employee who is scheduled for a performance appraisal deserves to be as prepared as you are. The appraisal interview is the employee's time to discuss any problems he is having on the job and also to ask your advice on career development. Asking an employee into your office at the last minute to meet for a performance appraisal not only is unfair, but it gives the impression that you are trying to avoid something.

The best way to prepare yourself and your employee for the meeting is for each of you to fill out complementary forms that cover two major areas:

1. *Job Analysis,* which is an evaluation and analysis of what the job entails. It identifies and assigns weight to each of the employee's areas of accountability.

2. *Performance/Work Habits Review,* which assigns a numerical rating for each characteristic.

You can create your own forms to best suit your needs, or you can use the samples in Chapter 3, where Figures 3-1 and 3-2 should give you a good starting point. Give your employee a copy of these forms three to five working days (weekends don't count) before the appraisal meeting and ask the employee to come to the meeting prepared to discuss the following:

- Job performance since the last review
- Personal career objectives
- Problems or concerns about the present job
- Things the employee would like to see change—personally and for the department in general
- Goals for improving future performance and productivity

The Job Analysis Form

On the job analysis form (see Figure 3-1 on page 20), the employee is asked to list all major job responsibilities and to give them a "weight," indicating the percentage of time on the job that the employee spends on each of those tasks. At the same time, you should fill out an identical form for the employee, giving your own perception of what the job entails. The first time you try this method, it can be quite a revelation just how differently you and your employees perceive their jobs. That's why it's important that you both agree on what should be evaluated. The job analysis form creates confirmation that both you and your employee are measuring the same tasks, responsibilities, and outcomes to the same degree. Of course, if you already have a job description on file, you and your employee could simply update the job description and later pass that update along to human resources for processing.

Let's listen in on what one supervisor learns when she tries this method for the first time:

Dorothy: Stanley, did you really mean to say that 50 percent of your time at work is spent helping your coworkers with their problems and questions?

Stanley: Yes, I did. I don't have to tell you that I've been with this department longer than anybody. People are always coming to me with questions, and I never turn them away. Sometimes, it does get hard to do my own work on time, but I manage, don't I?

Dorothy: Yes, you do. I wonder, though, if this is really the best use of your time. Let me ask you something: Do you find yourself answering the same types of questions over and over, or is it continually new problems?

Stanley: Actually, it's a lot of the same thing. Not to complain, but I find that some of the newer employees do use me as a crutch at times. They realize it's easier and faster to ask me how to do something than to figure it out on their own. Really, I don't mind.

By now, Dorothy is upset with herself for letting this situation go on without her knowledge, but she doesn't let it get the best of her. After she has some time to think about it, she comes up with an idea for utilizing Stanley's knowledge and improving productivity for all the department members involved.

Dorothy: Stanley, how would you feel about working with me to develop a training program—it might just take a few sessions—to get these people to start thinking for themselves? Not only would the rest of the department benefit, but it would be good managerial experience for you. I'd like you to help me lead the sessions, as well as choose what to include.

Stanley: It sounds like an interesting project, Dorothy. I'd be willing to give it a try. I also think that we could work up a type of resource manual that we can distribute to everyone in the department. What do you think?

Dorothy: I think it's a great idea. Thanks, Stanley. I'm feeling very optimistic about this venture.

The Performance/Work Habits Review Form

The job analysis form you give the employee is basically a blank sheet of paper with space for listing job responsibilities and tasks, the objectives of those tasks, and the percentage of time required (again, unless a job description already exists that could be updated). With mutual agreement reached regarding your perception of primary versus secondary responsibilities, it's time to focus on the individual's performance relative to those agreed-upon benchmarks.

The performance/work habits review form (see Figure 3-2 on page 24) should list those qualities that you believe pertain to that employee and her job. Both you and the employee independently rate the employee on a scale of one to five for each trait. (By contrast, you may ask your subordinate to provide narrative comments without a numerical ranking of any sort.) You may find the same form applicable for all of your employees, or you may adapt it to the individual being interviewed.

If you choose to adapt a standard model form to a particular employee's needs, be sure to emphasize the following three questions:

1. Have you (i.e., the employee) addressed your overall performance track record for the review period? Specifically, address any achievements that have resulted in increased revenues, decreased costs, or saved time. Why is our organization a better place for your having worked here? How would you grade yourself in terms of your work quality, reliability, interpersonal communication, and technical skills?

2. In what areas do you need additional support, structure, and direction? In other words, where can I, as your supervisor, provide you with additional support or resources in terms of acquiring new skills, strengthening your overall performance, or preparing you for your next move in career progression?

3. What are your performance goals for the upcoming review period? What measurable outcomes are necessary so that we will know that your goals have been reached?

Notice that in these three key areas, we shift the responsibility for objective performance analysis and goal determination back to the subordinate. That's where it should be for several reasons.

First, no one knows the essential aspects of the job better than the person doing the work.

Second, people will more readily assume responsibility for goals that they themselves create than those that are forced upon them.

Third, most employees will typically be more critical of their own performance than their bosses would ever be. Hence, their overly critical grading will give you, the supervisor, the chance to raise those grades and play coach and mentor rather than unilateral decision maker and disciplinarian.

Red-Flag Warning!

Well, if that third point above seems to fly in the face of your experience, you're not alone. Most managers filter this recommendation through their experiences with the worst employees they've ever had. Keep one simple point in mind, though: You give up no power or control at all by inviting your employees—even your most problematic subordinates—to assess themselves in advance of the meeting. In essence, you're the supervisor, you write the ultimate review, your opinion is final, and that simply doesn't change because you invite your subordinate to share in the process and volunteer information up front.

"Yeah," you say, "that's easy enough said. But what if my subordinate believes she's a five (stellar) and I believe she's a one (horri-ble)? Haven't I created unnecessary angst and conflict by inviting her to formally share in the evaluation process?"

Well, yes and no. Although it may appear at first that you're giving your subordinate the stick with which to draw a line in the sand, in reality, you've just given yourself an opportunity to discuss your differences in *perception*. Sharing your differences in per-ception gives you both an opportunity to discuss openly and objectively how you see the other person's performance or behav-ior—without negating his right to his own opinion or "making it personal." Feelings and perceptions aren't right or wrong, after all—they simply "are." Therefore, this could be just the tool you need to enter gently into a conversation that could otherwise be confrontational or nasty if left unaddressed.

Remember, be sure to give employees ample time to complete the forms and to think over what they would like to discuss at the appraisal interview. Then you are ready for step 2.

STEP 2: THE APPRAISAL INTERVIEW

Until now, you may have always begun your performance appraisal process by jumping right into step 2. Let's discuss the differences between that kind of appraisal and a truly productive performance appraisal. In Chapter 6, we talk about specific methods for conduct-ing the interview so that you'll be more comfortable in your role as performance reviewer.

Many supervisors start an appraisal interview by saying some-thing positive about the employee. What's wrong with that? Noth-ing at all. But we want to get beyond superficial compliments and discuss specific performance traits that we admire in the employee, as well as those traits that will help her improve and advance in her career.

Traditionally, employees view a performance appraisal as an or-deal they must go through before they can find out whether they will receive a salary increase, just how much that increase will be, and when and if they can ever expect to receive a promotion. By asking your employees to join you in a working session, you can shift that paradigm and change the expectations that your employees now have when they think about participating in a performance appraisal.

If this is new to your employees, it may take some time to get them to let their guard down and cooperate fully. But if you take the right approach, you should not encounter too much resistance. Think of it this way: You are asking employees to talk about their favorite topic—themselves.

Explain from the onset that you will not be discussing money issues at this initial meeting. Assure the employee that you will set up a separate meeting to discuss salary in the near future. That may take some time to sink in, but when it does, it frees you to talk solely about job performance and setting objectives for the future.

Because you have prepared your employee for the appraisal interview, there will be plenty to discuss. By filling out the job analysis and performance/work habit review forms, you have each provided yourselves with written evaluations that you can compare and discuss. In addition, the employee has been forced to think about what he is doing in the job and how that does or doesn't help meet ultimate career aspirations. Now, instead of spending the time you have with your employee justifying and explaining exactly how you came up with the amount of money in the proposed salary increase, you can talk about the quality of the employee's performance without worrying that your observations don't match up with a "high," "medium," or "low" increase. You have set the scene well for a genuinely productive, performance-focused meeting.

STEP 3: THE POST-APPRAISAL MEETING

Eventually, you will have to share the formalized, signed review and discuss salary issues with each of your employees. Although such a meeting should be separate from the appraisal interview (at least two or three days later), the final outcome should reflect what was decided on during that interview. For example, an interview that determined that the employee is ready for promotion should ideally be followed with either a promotion or a pledge that promotion will come as soon as it is permissible within company guidelines.

You must be careful not to promise anything that you won't be able to deliver. If you believe that the money you have to offer an employee will be a disappointment, be prepared to explain the company guidelines you followed.

Although salary may be the most important issue of the meeting in the employee's view, you should refocus the discussion and use it as an opportunity to review the objectives and goals you have both set and to sum up the overall performance rating score you have given the employee for the entire review period. You may also have some new responsibilities or assignments to give the employee at this meeting. Be sure to point out the connection between what was discussed at the appraisal interview and the new assignments. Let the employee know that you are available for assistance in learning any new responsibilities he will be taking on and that you will be meeting with the employee in the near future to discuss his progress in reaching newly determined goals. At that point and toward the end of the meeting, feel free to thank the employee for his contributions over the past year and share what the merit increase will be and when it will take effect.

CHAPTER 3

FACE-TO-FACE

———————————

N ow that we have identified the three major phases of the performance review, along with why you may want to change your method of preparing for and conducting employee performance appraisals, let's look at how best to handle such an interview when you finally come face-to-face.

A GOOD BEGINNING

Because most employees are nervous about what will be said at their performance reviews, you can help make the meeting more pleasant by trying to put the employee at ease right away:

Harvey: Come in and sit down, Matthew. Please don't look so nervous. We both know you're a solid performer and consistent contributor, and there are no major problems to bog us down, so this should be fairly painless!

Matthew: I sure hope so. . . .

Harvey: Okay, please try to relax. The purpose of this meeting is so that we can evaluate your performance together and also so that we can work together to plan the best path for your future. Have you brought the forms I asked you to fill out?

Matthew: Yes. I have them right here.

Harvey: Excellent. I've filled out the same forms. I want to compare what we've each written on the job analysis form, so we can see just how well we agree on what your major job responsibilities are.

Harvey is doing a fine job of beginning the interview. Right away, he has let Matthew know that the performance appraisal is going to be a positive one. Also, by acknowledging that there is natural tension, he has helped to dissipate some of that, too. By not attempting to cover up the purpose of the meeting with a lot of small talk, Harvey sets the tone for getting right down to the business at hand once he has promised Matthew that there is nothing to fear.

Using the job analysis form (see Figure 3-1) or an updated job description to begin the meeting is a good idea, too. Harvey and Matthew can talk about the objectives of the job before they get into a discussion on just how well Matthew is doing performance-wise. When Harvey and Matthew come to an area where they have given different weights, Harvey discusses it calmly and with an open mind, but he sticks to his agenda.

Harvey: I see that you've given new programming a weight of 15 percent and project support a weight of 25 percent. I've got the weights of those two switched here, with 25 percent for new programming and 15 percent for project support.

Matthew: Really? I wouldn't mind if that were the case because, frankly, I enjoy writing new programs. But it seems to me that I definitely spend more time on project support.

Harvey: If that's the case, let's consider changing that situation. I really need your talents used to develop new programs. In fact, I'd like to see the weight changed next time we meet to closer to 35 percent of your time spent on new and updated pro-

FIGURE 3-1. JOB ANALYSIS.

Employee: Matthew Gabe

Job Title: Programmer/Systems Analyst

Department: IT Systems and Programming

Responsibilities of Job	Functional Objectives	Weight
New programming	Create programs to increase IT efficiency.	25%
Project support	Update existing systems and programs.	15%
User assistance	Explain systems functions to users; adapt programs for user needs.	20%
Technical knowledge	Maintain current technical skills; master new hardware.	15%
Problem solving	Offer quick response to problems; maintain calm and professional attitude.	15%
Communications	Send and receive information effectively and in a timely manner.	10%

NOTE: This form is written for a very specific position, whereas the work habits form in Figure 3-2 can be used for just about any type of employee.

grams. Tell me, why do you think you spend so much time on support?

Matthew: I think it's because the users are always coming to me with bits and pieces of things they want to do or want to change. Maybe if there were better communication we could accomplish more at one time, and then the job of ongoing support would take less time and energy.

Harvey: That's a good thought. I agree with you, and I've got some ideas about improving those communications and would like to hear yours. I'll also be talking to the supervisor of the user department that you work with, to see if maybe we can work something out together.

Matthew: That would be great.

DISCUSS QUALITY OF PERFORMANCE

Once you and the employee have come to an agreement on just what the job entails and what the employee should be doing, you can then move on to the issue of quality of performance. This is where you can easily get into trouble. Unless you are careful about what you say to your employee, you can end up (1) causing resentment between the employee and yourself, (2) getting the wrong message across to the employee, or (3) saying nothing of major significance and wasting the opportunity to help the employee improve performance and grow in his career.

Harvey, for the most part, is pleased with Matthew's performance. He does have some suggestions for improvement, however.

Harvey: I'd like you to know, Matthew, that I think you're an excellent employee and that you are an asset to the programming department. Your programming technique has improved over the past six months. I was especially pleased with the way you handled the accounting program.

Matthew: Thanks. I worked hard on that program and I was happy with the way it turned out.

Harvey: If I asked you to pick one area where you felt you needed the most improvement, where would it be?

Assuming Matthew identifies interpersonal communication as his most-needed area of improvement, the conversation would continue as follows; otherwise, Harvey simply has to tell Matthew that, in his opinion as his manager, communication is what he'd like Matthew to focus on.

Harvey: As you said before, you notice that communications between programming and users is not always the most efficient.
I suspect part of it is that you still need to strengthen and develop your experience at getting to the bottom of what your
users need. I think that by consulting with them a little more
closely and by asking more questions before you start a project,
you may find that the results will be more satisfying. Does that
sound reasonable to you?

Matthew: I never thought of that before.

Harvey: Well, tell me if you could think of an example where a
deeper questioning approach up front may have saved time or
refocused your efforts. . . . What would you do differently in the
future if a client group approached you asking for your support
in any area that you weren't familiar with? What would you tell
the group members if they put undue pressure on you to problem solve something that was outside of your area of expertise?
What kinds of questions could you ask to initially assess the
challenge they were facing? You know, there is someone you
could learn a lot from in this regard. She really has a knack for
dealing with users and questioning her way to get at the core
problem. I'm talking about Joan Houlihan. How do you feel
about working with her for a while?

Matthew: What do you mean?

Harvey: I'm about to ask Joan to head a new project group for the
manufacturing research department. I'd like you to work on
that team and also to observe how Joan works with the users to
get the project under way. I can ask her to utilize you as associate group leader. In this way, you can be in on the inter-
departmental negotiations and you can also get some more
experience in project planning.

Matthew: That sounds very interesting.

Harvey: You understand that Joan would be in charge of leading
the group project, but that you would be her chief assistant.
This is for her benefit, too, of course. I think your technical

skills are the best in the group for this application, and I think you can help guide the other programmers on the team.

Matthew: Terrific. That answers my question about how I can get more leadership experience.

Harvey: I knew you would ask me about that, Matthew, and you have every right to. I do believe you have excellent leadership potential, but I want to make sure you can handle all aspects of project management when I ask you to take on your own team.

Harvey really has come prepared to this appraisal meeting. He has identified Matthew's weak point (user communications) and anticipated that Matthew would be eager to strive toward heading a project (a career objective that had been established in the previous appraisal). Harvey has already decided on a way to help both needs, and he presents it to Matthew in such a positive light that Matthew is, of course, pleased with being given the opportunity to achieve while learning.

Once you have given your overall impression of the employee's performance, discussing specific areas and incidents that concern you, you can turn to the performance/work habits review form (see Figure 3-2) and compare what each of you perceives to be the employee's strong and weak points. This form conveniently serves to summarize and pinpoint some of the things you may have just discussed. By identifying these traits on the form as "work habits," the employee can see how some of the specific behaviors you've already discussed can translate into a general impression of his competence.

If your employee has been honest in her self-evaluation, there should not be a great deal of disparity between your form and the employee's. If you gave a rating of 4 where an employee has rated herself a 3, it's not worth quibbling over. Point out that you agree the employee is doing well, and although there will always be room for improvement, you feel the work is more consistent with a grade of 4 rather than 3. Tell the employee what you like about what she is doing in this area. For example, "You consistently meet your deadlines. I appreciate that and hope that you can continue to be

FIGURE 3-2. PERFORMANCE/WORK HABITS REVIEW.

Employee: Matthew Gabe

Job Title: Programmer/Systems Analyst

Department: IT Systems and Programming

Check all items relevant to employee's position. Rate each item on a scale of one to five, by circling a number to the right of it.*

1 = Needs much improvement
2 = Needs some improvement
3 = Satisfactory
4 = Very good
5 = Excellent

Part I. General Work Habits

a.	Attendance/punctuality	1	2	3	4	5
b.	Meets deadlines	1	2	3	4	5
c.	Cooperates with coworkers	1	2	3	4	5
d.	Accepts suggestions	1	2	3	4	5
e.	Manages work schedule	1	2	3	4	5
f.	Uses equipment properly	1	2	3	4	5
g.	Prioritizes work well	1	2	3	4	5

Part II. Job Performance

a.	Quality of work	1	2	3	4	5
b.	Ability to solve problems	1	2	3	4	5
c.	Ability to use original ideas	1	2	3	4	5
d.	Communications abilities	1	2	3	4	5
e.	Time management	1	2	3	4	5
f.	Technical/professional knowledge	1	2	3	4	5
g.	Hands-on skills	1	2	3	4	5
h.	Interpersonal skills	1	2	3	4	5
i.	Ability to work on a team	1	2	3	4	5

NOTE: This form can be used for just about any type of employee, whereas the job analysis form in Figure 3-1 is written for a very specific position.

*These are standard ratings descriptions used by many companies today. At the end of Chapter 11, we will recommend alternative ratings descriptions that may better serve your company's and employees' needs.

so reliable." Remember to point out the positive marks you have given the employee and try to cite specific examples that influenced your giving the higher rating.

Concentrate on any areas where either of you has circled 1 or 2 when you talk about what areas need to be improved. For example, let's assume Matthew was having difficulty getting to meetings on time, but he wasn't aware of how much of an impact it had made on his supervisor:

Harvey: I've only given you one rating of 1, Matthew, and that's in punctuality. I've spoken to you a number of times about getting to meetings on time, but I still see you coming in late a full ten to twenty minutes after the meetings have begun—that's a lot, Matthew.

Matthew: I know. But I always meet my deadlines; I always get my work done. . . . I stay late if I have to. I just find it hard to get to client meetings all over the campus on time. Does it really matter if I'm a few minutes late as long as the end-user is satisfied with the work we've done?

Harvey: It *is* important, because you don't work in a vacuum, Matthew. When you arrive late and force others to either wait for you or repeat things for you, you show a lack of respect for their time. We're in an internal client–focused business, and we have to vie for these clients' business so that they don't look outside the company for their IT projects. Is there a specific reason why you can't seem to make it to user meetings on time?

Matthew: No, but. . . . What about Wendy? She shows up at a lot of client meetings later than I do.

Harvey: Well, we're not really here to discuss Wendy. Just so you know, though, she has a different role and scope than you in client meetings and typically notifies her supervisor in advance if she can't arrive on time. Still, this is about you, so, again, is there any particular reason why you're having difficulty getting to your client meetings on time?

Matthew: No. Well, I'm just not a naturally early riser, and if I start off my day late first thing in the morning, I tend to run late throughout the day.

Harvey: I wish we could accommodate everybody's inner clock, but we can't, Matthew. I have to tell you that you really need to discipline yourself to arrive at work on time. I'd hate for a relatively minor infraction to stand in the way of your advancement.

Matthew: I understand what you're saying. I'll do a better job at getting to user meetings on time from now on.

Harvey finally comes down hard on Matthew about his late arrivals. Although he pointed out the infractions when they happened, Harvey waits until the appraisal to really make an impression on Matthew. If you realize that you've failed to change your employee's behavior through daily interaction, you can use the performance appraisal to finally get your point across. After all, there is something about seeing a shortcoming on paper that makes it impossible to ignore.

ASK FOR INPUT

A productive performance appraisal allows for give-and-take between you and your employee. Ask the employee how she feels about the quality of her own performance and what she would like to change (see further discussion of this subject in Chapter 4). Harvey broaches the subject in this way:

Harvey: Matthew, have you given any thought to your strengths and weaknesses? What are the strengths that you really want to leverage? What skills would you like to try to improve? What areas would you like to learn more about?

Matthew: Well, I'm pretty satisfied with my technical programming ability, but I would like to learn some additional languages. I would also like to improve my proficiency on other hardware and software systems.

Perhaps because Harvey has asked Matthew to come prepared to talk about skills development, he had an easy time in getting Matthew to identify the areas he would like to work on. When employees are not accustomed to thinking about their future career prospects, it can be a lot more difficult to get the conversation going.

WATCH WHAT YOU SAY—AND HOW YOU SAY IT

Can you remember sitting at a performance review and hearing your supervisor say things that made you want to start whistling and looking at the ceiling? It probably brought back memories of the lectures your parents or teachers gave you when your behavior came under scrutiny.

Too often, we revert to old, tried-and-true phrases to express ourselves. In other words, we use clichés. When we let this happen, we generally lose other people's attention and cause them to doubt whether we are really attuned to them as individuals.

Here are some of the more common clichés—both negative and positive—embraced by supervisors at performance appraisal times. The first three examples show how you can express the same ideas in a more personal way by citing specific behavior.

Cliché 1

"You're not living up to your potential."

More Personal: "I was confident that you had enough experience in this area to handle this assignment, Amy. Why do you think you've had trouble getting the work done correctly?"

Cliché 2

"You make very good use of your time."

More Personal: "I'm pleased with the way I see you organize your workload, Richard. I was especially impressed with how you were able to finish that last assignment without having to work overtime.''

Cliché 3

"I feel sometimes your behavior is very immature."

More Personal: "The way you handled that complaint by Mr. Smith was inappropriate, Sharon. You have to control your temper and concentrate on solving the problem. Instead, you seemed to take his complaint personally, and you responded defensively instead of helpfully."

Now try some on your own. Here are several more examples of overused expressions. Try to come up with more original ways to get your message across. Write down your ideas in the space provided. Because it's a performance appraisal, remember to cite specific behavior so that your remarks are instructive to the employee.

Cliché 4

"You need to improve your productivity."

More Personal:

_____

_____

_____

_____

Cliché 5

"You get along well with others."

More Personal:

_____

_____

_____

_____

Cliché 6

"Your skills are not up to par."

More Personal:

_____

_____

_____

_____

Cliché 7

"You're not trying to do your best."

More Personal:

_____

_____

_____

_____

Cliché 8

"You're a pleasure to supervise."

More Personal:

_____

_____

_____

_____

Cliché 9

"You have to prove yourself before I can give you any more responsibility."

More Personal:

_____

_____

_____

_____

Cliché 10

"I wish I could do more to help you, but my hands are tied."

More Personal:

_____

_____

_____

_____

SETTING THE SCENE

To give an appraisal interview your undivided attention and to make your employee as comfortable as possible, take the time to set the scene for a productive meeting. Use the following checklist to make sure you haven't forgotten anything:

Checklist for Setting the Scene

❑ Arrange to have all calls forwarded to a receptionist or voice mail and visitors diverted.

❑ Make sure you have scheduled enough time for the meeting.

❑ Clear your desk of any extraneous papers or files that will get in the way of your working on the desk with forms and papers.

❑ Make sure the temperature level in your office is comfortable—neither too cold nor too warm.

❑ Have a pitcher of water and cups handy, if possible.

❑ Put away anything you tend to fidget with, such as rubber bands and paper clips.

❑ Have all necessary paperwork and forms ready.

❑ Provide the employee with a comfortable chair.

PART II

HOW TO MAKE IT HAPPEN: ADVANCE PREPARATIONS

CHAPTER 4

PLAN FOR THE FUTURE

Perhaps the most important part of any performance appraisal is the part that is, quite often, either left out completely or given short shrift. Yet it can make the difference between a productive meeting and a superficial discussion. We are, of course, referring to the employee development and career objectives portion of the appraisal.

Almost every employee has hopes and aspirations beyond her present job. For some people, these hopes remain distant wishes. But for those lucky enough to have the right supervisor and the necessary motivation, career objectives can become obtainable goals.

During each performance appraisal you should work with the employee to come up with a list of long-term and short-term career goals. Then, at the next appraisal meeting, you should evaluate what progress has been made toward these goals, what new directions the employee's career has taken, and together you can decide if and how the employee's strategic plans should be changed.

HOW SUPERVISORS CAN HELP

Let's look at two examples of how supervisors can help employees plan for their career futures. Of course, many companies don't have defined career paths that lead from one position or title to the next after a specific period of time. However, even if your company can't offer a specific promotional path, you could still focus on helping your subordinates add new skills to their resumes or reinvent their positions in light of your department's changing needs.

In the first example, Kathy, the employee, has a definite idea in mind about her next promotion. In the second example, Kathy looks for more lateral types of responsibilities to strengthen her overall skill base. Watch how Sara, her supervisor, leads her skillfully through these two alternatives.

Sara: Kathy, when discussing the quality of your overall performance, the areas where you excel and the areas where you'd like additional support and assistance make up the crux of the annual performance review. But equally important is your development plan, where the focus lies more on your longer-term career goals.

   Although I can't promise promotional or vertical opportunities at our firm at any given time, it might be worth our time to consider your next move in career progression and what we could do now to prepare to get you there. Likewise, if vertical growth doesn't appear to be an option at this point, let's talk about assuming lateral responsibilities or otherwise broadening your overall skill set. Have you given some thought to that?

Role Play #1

Kathy: Actually, I've been giving this a lot of thought—especially since you asked me to work on it last week. As an employment assistant, I'm supporting our recruiters with drafting and running online recruitment ads, screening resumes, initiating telephone interviews, checking references, and running background checks.

In essence, I'm pretty much doing everything they're doing shy of making the offer and closing the deal. I'd very much like to be promoted to recruiter since I'm probably doing 80 percent of the job anyway.

Sara: That's a very realistic goal, especially since that would be the next logical move for you anyway, both on paper and in terms of your longer-term goals. Now let me ask you this: How much time do you think it would take to reach that next title, and what would you need to do from this point to strengthen your qualifications for the recruiter role once it becomes available?

Kathy: Well, I'd hope that something would become available in the next six to twelve months, and I'm already looking into attending a recruiting and selection course offered by the local college.

Sara: Good. Then you're off to a good start! Let's fine-tune this idea a bit, though, so that we're both on the same page in terms of the qualifications you'd need as well as the focus of your efforts. First, I think six to twelve months is a bit optimistic. I don't believe we'll have any additions to head count in the next year or two, so the opening will only surface if someone leaves. Therefore, a twelve- to twenty-four-month window of expectation may be more realistic. Does that make sense to you?

Kathy: Oh, okay. I didn't realize it could take that long, and I didn't know that I couldn't be promoted until someone else left. I'm glad you clarified that, but isn't there such a thing as being promoted in place?

Sara: Yes and no, Kathy. Promotions in place can happen, but in the case of our department, to do so would throw our structure out of place. We have three employment assistants supporting six recruiters. If we promote one of those employment assistants into a recruiter role without being able to add any other head count at the employment assistant level, it would put too much pressure on the remaining employment assistants. Do you follow my logic?

Kathy: Oh, I see.

Sara: In addition, Kathy, I'd recommend that you take two classes at the local junior college rather than one. Recruitment and selection is the most logical course for you at this point, I agree. But you'll also need to take a course on the legal aspects of human resources management. In other words, you'll really want to have a better understanding of the laws that govern the workplace. This way, you're not just seeing recruitment and selection in and of itself, but as a part of a greater whole. And since both of these courses are job related, we can apply for tuition reimbursement using the company's educational assistance plan. And there's one more thing: I'd like for you to sit in on some employment offers and get a feel for the nature of the negotiation that goes on. This way you'll have live experience to complement your course work. Once you've seen how deals can go awry for a myriad of reasons, you'll be much better suited for the recruiter role once one opens up. Tell me how that sounds to you initially. . . .

Now, let's see how Sara can help Kathy even if Kathy is unsure of what she wants to do next with her career.

Role Play #2

Kathy: Gee, I've been thinking about my development plan, but I'm really not sure where I go from here. I just know that I want to be able support our department in as many ways as possible, and I know that I'd like to gain exposure to the other side of the house—compensation, benefits, and human resources systems.

Sara: Well, let's think. As I've said, your performance has been excellent and you show a lot of potential. What aspects of those areas that you mentioned most interest you?

Kathy: Well . . . I find compensation really fascinating. When we determine how much we should offer a candidate, we have a preapproved salary range, we know what the candidate is currently earning, and then we have to do an internal equity study to find out what our existing employees in that department currently make. Once we examine the whole compensation picture, then we can determine a fair offer. But as much as we'd like to bring in new hires at a lower salary than existing employees, sometimes we just can't do that because the market for a particular skill set has gone through the roof. That's fascinating stuff! And I also want to gain a better understanding of incentive stock options and other long-term perks that might not show themselves in a weekly paycheck.

Sara: Okay, so it sounds like compensation is your primary focus. You also mentioned benefits and HR systems. . . .

Kathy: Yeah, those are great too, but my more immediate interest lies in compensation.

Sara: So how would you see yourself learning more about compensation shy of picking up a book at the library?

Kathy: Well, I know the local junior college offers a number of human resources–related courses, including compensation. Maybe I could enroll in that.

Sara: That's a great idea. I also think you'll be eligible to participate in our tuition reimbursement program since that would be considered a job-related course. You just gave me another great idea, though. How about if we set you up to work with our compensation team on a short-term basis? You'd get exposure to all areas of comp, not just what goes on in the preemployment offer stage of recruitment. And that, in turn, would give you a much more global view of the world of compensation— some practical training to go along with your studies. How does that sound?

By picking Kathy's brain a bit and asking her to think about what she likes in her job, Sara is able to bring out what Kathy's ideal career goal would be—whether focused on a vertical or horizontal assumption of new responsibilities. In the first role play, you'll notice that Sara had to temper Kathy's ambitions a bit: Kathy was under the impression that she could be promoted in place simply because she was handling many recruiter responsibilities. Sara deftly changed Kathy's time line expectation from six to twelve months to one to two years, and she offered Kathy hands-on experience that would strengthen her credentials and meet her immediate need for greater responsibilities.

In the second example, Sara helped Kathy focus her three areas of interest down to one (compensation), and Sara then offered to give Kathy greater insight and exposure into that one area of expertise. In both cases, Kathy's expectations were aligned with departmental needs, her requests for additional education and exposure were met, and the chances of retaining Kathy over the long haul were increased. That's not a bad return on investment of Sara's time . . . especially since this newly invigorated, highly motivated staff member will then be able to provide utility support in more than one area of Sara's department!

Remember that training is the glue that binds someone to your company. Giving staff members the opportunity to add new skills to their resumes, broaden their global viewpoint, or focus their career development efforts in a particular direction is what makes learning and working fun. In short, your subordinates will less likely be "recruiters' bait" waiting to jump ship for the next opportunity that comes their way if they feel you are interested in their career growth and development. That, more than anything, makes for loyalty among subordinates and stellar reputations of leadership among managers.

WORKING OUT A PLAN

Once you've identified an employee's future career objective, you can work out a plan of action that will include gaining experience, obtaining training, and whatever else is needed. An example of a job objectives worksheet is shown in Figure 4-1 on page 40. Take the employee through the plan step by step:

1. Examine the list of objectives that was identified at the previous interview. Evaluate the progress the employee has made in reaching these objectives.

2. Determine which objectives need further work. Discuss what obstacles have prevented the employee from reaching any objectives. Decide if time frames set for reaching objectives need to be adjusted.

3. Discuss objectives that have been reached. How have the employee's skills and performance improved as a result? What are the next levels the employee will now aspire to reach?

4. Discuss whether the employee's ultimate career objective remains the same or has changed. How will this circumstance affect the objectives that have already been set?

5. Set new objectives for the upcoming year. Discuss what the employee needs to learn to reach these objectives and how the employee can obtain the knowledge and experience needed.

6. Assign responsibility for reaching these goals. Let the employee know to what extent you will help him and what the employee must do independently.

7. Pick a starting point. One of the most common reasons that "new objective lists" aren't acted upon is that the employee is left in the end with such a large task that he ends up doing nothing about moving ahead with the goals. Therefore, if you can decide together on a first step that will start the employee toward reaching a tangible goal, you have a much better chance of seeing the employee achieve success.

8. Make plans to meet again. Agree to meet with the employee in one to two months (but no more than three) to evaluate his progress.

COUNSELING THE PLATEAUED EMPLOYEE

Eventually, some employees reach a point where they have risen as far as they are likely to go within their organization. Whether they

FIGURE 4-1. JOB OBJECTIVES WORKSHEET.

Ultimate Goal: To become a corporate recruiter

Interim Goal	Plan of Action	Progress Made
1. Become more knowledgeable about recruitment and selection.	Take course on recruitment and employee selection at local college. Attend in-house HR training programs sponsored by our training and development department.	
2. Gain experience in all aspects of the hiring process, including candidate sourcing, interviewing, reference checking, and salary offers.	Develop a network with corporate recruiters at other divisions across the country and reach out to recruiters at competitor firms in town to better understand our marketplace and gather more resources.	
3. Learn how recruitment interfaces with compensation, benefits, Human Resource Information Systems (HRIS), and on-boarding.	Read summary plan description for our 401(k) and other literature relating to stock options, restricted stock shares, and other long-term incentive perks.	
4. Understand how contingency and retained search works to compete more effectively with these outsourced staffing options.	Learn how to negotiate contingency and retained search fees, fee guarantees, and refund periods. Read book on outsourcing HR functions.	

lack the ability, skills, or education to achieve more, or whether they have simply found the position that suits them best, counseling these employees during appraisal interviews requires different tactics from the supervisor. The aim in this case is to keep these employees motivated and interested in their work.

To reach what we call a *plateau,* an employee must attain a high degree of proficiency in his position. Chances are there is little need to improve the employee's job skills and the employee has a great deal of experience in all aspects of the job. If the employee does not wish to move ahead and, indeed, is truly best positioned where he is, are performance appraisals then a waste of time?

Obviously, we have to answer that assumption with a no. For this type of employee, the performance appraisal becomes more of a renewal of commitment and statement of purpose than a session in which you work on planning goals for the next step up the ladder. But that doesn't mean that the appraisal cannot be valuable.

The employee who knows he is staying in his current position is probably especially in need of positive reinforcement. Because the work may no longer be very challenging, the employee may have forgotten how essential it is, or he may not realize that you appreciate being able to depend on him for consistent and high-quality work.

And just because the employee is not looking to change positions doesn't mean that he can never take on any new roles in the department. Are there any new responsibilities the department is taking on in which this employee can become involved? The performance appraisal would be a perfect time to discuss such possibilities.

One role that plateaued employees traditionally enjoy is that of trainer or mentor to newer employees. If individuals are paired well, this type of arrangement can add new dimensions to the employee's job that will increase his morale and job satisfaction. It can certainly be rewarding to teach and train another employee—as long as the senior employee receives recognition for his efforts.

Employees who have been with their departments for a long time usually have a very good understanding of how things are run. They can be ideal for delegating some of the more routine supervisory tasks, thereby freeing up some of your own time for more pressing matters.

The important thing to remember during an appraisal for this type of employee is to stress the positive and let the employee know how much you count on him. Don't be afraid to ask if the employee has any ideas on how the job can be made more challenging, or if there are any responsibilities that are outside his current position that are of interest. Consider asking, "How has your role changed in light of our company's or department's changing needs?" or "What areas of interest, if any, would you like to consider exploring at this point?" After all, our most tenured workers often have the most insightful recommendations for reinventing the work flow and maximizing efficiencies. Still, we have to respect that some people enjoy their routines and aren't necessarily looking to take on added responsibilities of any sort. What's important is that you simply ask, because that way you show you care. And caring, by definition, ensures open communication, recognition, and appreciation.

You may be surprised that when you get a good discussion going, there is still some room for change on the employee's agenda.

CHAPTER 5

DOCUMENT, DOCUMENT, DOCUMENT

Have you ever sat down to work on an evaluation of one of your employees for an upcoming performance appraisal and had your mind go blank? Of course, you know the employee well. You know what he has been working on for the past four weeks and . . . what else? What did go on with that employee in the past six months or a year?

Well, you should *never* experience this type of anxiety again because a mandatory component of productive performance appraisals is that you keep an up-to-date journal on each of your employees. The buzzword here is "documentation."

You may well agree with documentation of employee performance in theory, but in practice you think you just don't need it. Let's look at some of the reasons often cited and tackle them one at a time:

Excuse 1: "I have a very good memory. I won't forget what my employees do; therefore, it's a waste of my time."

Fact: Even people who have a good memory will remember most sharply those events that are most recent. This is referred to as the "recency effect." Recent minor events may have greater rating influence than older, major events because of the amount of time that has elapsed. To properly evaluate an employee's performance, you need to look at the entire work period, not just the last two months.

Excuse 2: "I have only a few employees. You're referring to supervisors who have larger departments than mine."

Fact: No. We mean all supervisors regardless of how many employees they manage. "Critical incidence diaries" or "performance logs" help you maintain and categorize significant achievements, letters of recommendation, and samples of inferior work product so that you can justify your evaluation of the individual's performance objectively and fairly.

Excuse 3: "It takes too long. I have better ways to spend my time."

Fact: This isn't something that you have to add to your daily or weekly activities list. Simply commit to dropping significant performance information into a folder so that it's available in the future. An exception: Many employers follow the rule of "document, document, document" to a fault. Remember that the documentation, in and of itself, can rapidly become outdated data. The true value of the process lies in sharing the information with your subordinate immediately and making it a learning event. More important, if you believe the information might possibly result in formal discipline or even termination, bring it to your HR department's attention immediately for prompt handling. If too much time occurs between the actual event and your reporting it to HR, then your delay may severely limit your company's ability to handle the matter appropriately.

Excuse 4: "My employees will resent my writing about them. They'll think I'm a spy."

Fact: The journal is meant to document every type of performance—good and bad. In fact, supervisors who keep journals tend to evaluate employees more favorably because they are reminded of good decisions that are easily forgotten or overshadowed by an isolated error.

Excuse 5: "I hate to put things like that in writing. It could come back to haunt me later."

Fact: The only reason to feel this way is if you don't know what is appropriate to include in an employee performance journal. That information is covered in this chapter.

START AT THE BEGINNING

Employee journals should include two types of information: incident reports, which document specific events that involve the employee; and progress reports, in which the supervisor comments on and evaluates work in progress. The sample forms in Figures 5-1 and 5-2 can be adapted for your own use.

Ideally, an employee's performance journal is started as soon as she is hired. Include in the journal the employee's original job application and resume and some thoughts you had that led you to make the hiring decision. Also include the written job description for which the employee was hired.

If you have never kept a journal to document employee performance, now is the time to create one for each of your employees, regardless of how long they have been with you. Don't be upset if you don't have the job application and resume. It's not vital

FIGURE 5-1. SAMPLE EMPLOYEE PERFORMANCE JOURNAL—INCIDENT REPORT FORM.

Employee Name: _____

Position: _____

Date Hired: _____

Starting Salary: _____

Date	Event	Action Taken	Result	Follow-Up
_____	_____	_____	_____	_____

FIGURE 5-2. SAMPLE EMPLOYEE PERFORMANCE JOURNAL—PROGRESS REPORT FORM.

Date: _____

Current Projects: _____

_____

Evaluation of Work, Problems, Successes, etc.

_____

_____

_____

_____

that you go back to the very beginning. It is helpful, though, if you can, to list all positions the employee has held in the organization and to include a formal job description of each one. Even if the employee has been with the organization for many years, it can give you some interesting insight to read descriptions of each position the individual has held. Likewise, it is interesting for the employee to read those descriptions and see just how far he has progressed over the years.

The initial setup of each performance journal may be a little time-consuming, depending on the number of employees you supervise. But once that is done, keeping up with performance documentation need not take very much time. By remaining diligent in your documentation, you will end up with a journal for each employee that truly tells a story about how that employee functions in the workplace. It will be an invaluable tool for your performance appraisals. Make sure that your direct reports keep performance journals on their immediate subordinates (i.e., your "extended reports") as well.

DOCUMENTATION SERVES AS PROTECTION, TOO

In addition to its usefulness in employee evaluations, your journal can be used for your own protection, and protection for your company, if you are accused of bias or improper behavior by an employee or by another manager, especially if a lawsuit is brought forth. Any incidents that are out of the ordinary or that involve a significant clash of tempers or personalities should be included in the documentation.

In fact, to further protect yourself, you should ask the employee involved in an altercation or unusual incident to read your documentation of the event and sign it, to indicate that the facts are correct. This step will prevent such incidents from being distorted at a later date. It will also keep you from overemphasizing the incident at a performance review if your documentation is accurate.

As a litmus test, employ a "fairness test" of sorts to performance appraisals by asking, "If I was given a corporate mandate to cut head count by 20 percent, could I rely on the documented performance appraisals in my subordinates' files to determine who stays and who should go?"

Remember that as a general rule of thumb companies rely on multiple considerations when having to decide who is the least qualified staff member to assume the remaining job duties after a layoff. Some of those considerations include tenure, education, certifications, absentee record, performance reviews, and progressive disciplinary records. Now just place yourself in the shoes of a plaintiff attorney who is accusing you and your company of wrongfully selecting her client (i.e., your ex-employee) for layoff. The lawyer's argument may sound like this:

"Your honor, my client, their ex-employee, had more tenure than anyone else in the department. She had an excellent track record in terms of her annual performance reviews, and the only reason she was chosen to be laid off versus other members of the team was because of her [fill in the blank in terms of protected categories: age, sex, color, etc.]."

Now you know for a fact that that portrayal of the situation is simply not true: This individual suffered from an entitlement mentality, always showed an "attitude" when dealing with you, even in front of other subordinates, and the other members of the team tended to avoid her as well.

Of course, these may all be valid facts and perceptions, but unfortunately, you never reflected those issues in the former employee's performance reviews. What you did, instead, was give her an overall rating of 3 (Satisfactory or Meets Expectations) rather than 5 (Excellent or Outstanding), which is the score that all your other subordinates received. You assumed that she would somehow get the message that she was the weakest player on the team because she only received a work performance grade of 3.

Unfortunately, performance reviews are absolute, not relative. The fact that she scored a 3 told her that she met all company expectations. Whether she knew that everyone else on the team got a 5 was irrelevant. Your formal documentation that she met expectations was all she needed to confirm that her performance was acceptable. As such, her attorney could argue that the individual was denied workplace due process and is consequently entitled to reinstatement plus back wages or other damages.

This example is all too common in corporate America, where well-intentioned supervisors take the path of least resistance by inflating grades to avoid confrontation. Fortunately, there's a simple way to get around it: If you tend to overinflate grades or give everyone on your team the same grades year in and year out (e.g., everyone gets a 3 or everyone gets a 5), then realize that you may not be doing yourself or your company any favors. Your lack of differentiation wouldn't allow you to pass the fairness test in that your documentation record doesn't distinguish between acceptable and unacceptable employee performance. And that in turn means that the court or arbitrator may substitute its decision-making authority for yours in terms of deciding who should have gotten laid off or who should have had the right to be retained after the reduction in force.

To pass the fairness test, simply "force rank" your employees every time you sit down to prepare their performance reviews. If you have five subordinates, list as no. 1 the person you simply couldn't live without; your department or company would suffer the most damage if this person were to leave the company. Then list as no. 5 the person who, for whatever reason, wouldn't compromise your department at all if he were to leave your company.

Now here's the catch: If you suspect that a person won't make it through the upcoming year because of performance or conduct challenges, then document in the Overall Score section of the performance review that the individual isn't meeting expectations. This notation will create the appropriate performance record that will give you and your company the most discretion when determining who gets to remain on the team after a layoff is announced.

Furthermore, keep in mind that each performance review has individual categories as well as an Overall Score. Although your grades and narrative comments in the individual categories are important, the most important grade comes at the end of the review in the Overall Score section. That's the score that attorneys, judges, and arbitrators pay most attention to, so don't feel safe if you give subpar scores in individual performance categories while still showing that the individual meets the company's overall standards. Such logic could come back to haunt you.

As always, when in doubt, seek the advice of your company's HR department or qualified legal counsel. Your up-front investment may pay for itself a hundredfold when you suspect that a subordinate is inclined to sue.

DON'T SPRING "NEGATIVE SURPRISES"

Furthermore, a cardinal rule of productive performance appraisals is "no negative surprises." Any new information that the employee learns about for the first time in the annual, documented performance review will smack of unfairness and sabotage. Still, there may be times when new information must be surfaced in an annual review. When that's the case, be sure to document in the review itself that the information hasn't been brought to the employee's attention beforehand. For example, begin your narrative comment like this: "I recognize that we haven't formally discussed [state matter]. However, I feel that it is appropriate to bring this issue to your attention during this annual performance review because . . . ."

Truth be told, if something totally new needs to be surfaced for the first time on the annual review form, then you probably didn't do a thorough enough job on your end communicating with your subordinate during the review period. With this up-front acknowledgment, however, you can justify your reasoning and avoid leaving your subordinate feeling like he's been blindsided.

DOCUMENTATION KEEPS YOU OBJECTIVE

Maintaining documentation of your employees' performance is not only very handy when you are faced with the difficult decision of laying off a department member; it's also useful when choosing an employee for promotion. Before making any promotion recommendation, it is best to go over the documentation on all employees concerned in the decision. If you have done a thorough and consistent job in terms of honestly assessing and documenting your subordinates' performance, the documentation can help you make a choice based on actual performance and experience, rather than personality. Take Carol's case, for instance.

Carol supervised a group of six salespeople for a growing toy manufacturer. Although base salaries of the six were the same, the sales staff earned different amounts according to the commissions they received. For that reason, there was competition among them as to who would be given the most desirable territory.

When a new sales territory opened up, Carol was torn over which employee would get it. The region bordered on territories covered by three of her people.

Mark was the most flamboyant of the group. His charming manners and good looks helped a great deal in pitching sales. He knew the market and boasted in the office that he placed the product in 75 percent of the stores he visited.

Erica was quieter, but her sales record was solid. She was consistent in bringing in orders, but she was modest. When Mark boasted of a new sale, she just smiled and congratulated him. She never shared news of her own successes.

Jeffrey did well, but at first sight you might be surprised that he sold toys. A rather humorless man, his demeanor never hinted at the possibility that he ever had any fun.

At lunch with another sales manager, Evan, who knew all the members of Carol's department, Carol discussed the decision she would soon have to make about the new sales territory:

Evan: Between the three, it barely seems to be a contest. Mark has it all over the other two. He could sell ice to the Alaskans, couldn't he?

Carol: Actually, it's very interesting that you say that. I used to believe that myself, but about eight months ago I decided to keep a performance journal on each of my salespeople. I was reading them over yesterday and found it pretty insightful.

Evan: What do you need something like that for? Don't their sales figures speak for themselves?

Carol: Not really. You have to take into consideration the territories they work and the different products they are each asked to sell. It's not always as easy to judge as picking the highest order placer. Besides, I've included additional information in these journals.

Evan: Like what?

Carol: Well, like how many days are spent on the road and how often they are in the office doing paperwork or whatever. I've also kept track of expense accounts, and I've included feedback I get on each of the employees from clients.

Evan [curious now]: Really? So what did you find?

Carol: I found that Mark is not the top salesman he purports to be. He's good, but we have someone who is better.

Evan [guessing]: That quiet Erica?

Carol: No. It's Jeffrey. All things considered, he deserves the new territory the most.

Evan: Stone Face? Who'd have thought?

Carol: Please, Evan, watch what you say.

Evan: Sorry, it's just that from the looks of things, you'd never pick him as the top producer.

Carol: I agree. But when I compared everything about the three, his position on top came out very clear. Now the hard part will be breaking the news.

Evan: Don't worry about it. If you've really got the facts to back up your decision, you're in good shape.

Carol: You know, you're right. Those journals really did come in handy, after all.

It's not hard to see how Carol could have made a different choice if she had not had the performance journals to rely on. Personality, bragging, even an employee's looks can have a strong effect when you must make a choice among people. Basing most choices on the facts is a safe and fair way to decide, and accurate, appropriate documentation will be very helpful to you.

To make the determination on what information should be included in a journal and what should not, take the quiz on the Ins and Outs of Journal Keeping. Not everything you see belongs in an employee performance journal.

INS AND OUTS OF JOURNAL KEEPING

If you believe your employee performance journal should include a specific type of information, check "In"; if not, check "Out." Compare your answers against those in the key at the end of the quiz.

1. Data on employee attendance, lateness, extended lunches.   ___ In   ___ Out

2. Rumors circulated about employee.   ___ In   ___ Out

3. Data on what tasks the employee works on, including project names, coworkers, outside contacts, and any feedback on employee relevant to job performance.   ___ In   ___ Out

4. Unsupported complaints by others against employee.   ___ In   ___ Out

5. Data on overtime worked and/or offered to employee.   __ In   __ Out

6. Any disciplinary actions or verbal warnings given to employee.   __ In   __ Out

7. Personal comments about employee, including any
   judgments about fashion, hairstyle, or how "good" or "bad"
   an employee's appearance may be.   __ In   __ Out

8. Facts about employee's personal lifestyle—whether employee
   is married or single, a parent or not.   __ In   __ Out

9. Noteworthy successes or failures of employee on the job.   __ In   __ Out

10. Training courses taken and/or offered to employee.   __ In   __ Out

11. Your opinion on what employees should do regarding their
    careers.   __ In   __ Out

12. Your impressions of the quality of employee's work, including
    facts about work that support your opinions.   __ In   __ Out

13. Your interpretation or analysis of "why the employee does
    what he does."   __ In   __ Out

14. Details of discussions with the employee about any policy
    infractions.   __ In   __ Out

ANSWERS

1. In; 2. Out; 3. In; 4. Out; 5. In; 6. In; 7. Out; 8. Out; 9. In; 10. In; 11. Out; 12. In; 13. Out; 14. In.

The bottom line is that when you keep an employee performance journal, stick to the facts. Your personal feelings or opinions about the employee may remain with you, but they should not be written down in the journal. Anything that borders on a personal comment or one that can be construed to show prejudice or bias should be kept out of the journal.

When documenting disruptive or damaging incidents, include as many of the facts as you can. In cases of disciplinary action, write up exactly what transpired, what action was taken, and what was discussed. Then have the employee sign the documentation for the record.

CHAPTER 6

PREPARE YOURSELF

W e won't deny that conducting performance appraisals can indeed set you up to feel ill at ease. It's understandable, after all, that you may be uncomfortable passing judgment on the people you work with every day and how well they perform their jobs. Granted, your position as manager gives you the right to do it, but it's human nature to squirm a little.

However, if you've taken the time to prepare carefully for each performance appraisal you hold with your employees, you don't have to feel discomfited. This chapter includes two checklists you'll want to use to make sure that you are ready before you start your meeting.

If you've taken the advice from this book and given the employee a self-evaluation form, as well as filled out a copy of the same form yourself, you'll have taken the first step to make the meeting less awkward. Why? Because you've set up some automatic structure for the session.

Going over the job analysis form with the employee allows you to discuss the work that the employee does on a daily basis. If the two of you disagree on the relative importance or volume of specific job aspects, it will come out now, and it will also give you the opportunity to discuss any problems the employee is having performing the various job responsibilities.

AVOID ERRORS IN PERFORMANCE REVIEWS

If you think back to what you've most disliked about some of the performance appraisals you've been subjected to yourself, you can help make sure to avoid the errors of those who have gone before you. Some common mistakes that supervisors make when giving performance reviews are:

■ *Assuming a Patronizing Attitude.* Supervisors who come across as if they know exactly what is best for the employee in terms of career growth and development, without asking about the employee's personal goals, will generally be tuned out. In fact, the employee is apt to feel resentful and take the opposite of any advice given. Therefore, make sure this meeting is a two-way communication process, and approach it in a *listening* as well as *telling* mode.

■ *Stressing the Negative.* Some supervisors believe it is their responsibility to point out everything the employee is doing wrong. The performance review is the appropriate time to discuss real problems, but it is also imperative that you talk about what the employee is doing right. And think about your complaints before you speak. Are they really significant? Remember that anything negative you say during a performance appraisal will have a lasting effect. Make sure it's worth it.

■ *Lacking Information.* Supervisors who don't know what their employees are working on or what problems they are having are actually caught off guard at performance appraisals. This problem can be solved in a twofold manner: First, keep performance logs or critical incidents diaries on all your subordinates. Second, spend time reviewing the individual's self-evaluation before engaging in the actual performance review discussion. You'll have a chance to see what your subordinate feels is important by way of accomplishments over the past review period, areas that will require your additional support, and initial thoughts on the employee's development plan.

■ *Comparing Employees.* If at all possible, leave other employees out of the discussion. Talking about how good other employees are compared to the person being reviewed is asking for trouble. It is not a productive technique and unnecessarily creates feelings of resentment among coworkers. Again, it is totally acceptable to "rank order" your subordinates in terms of performance and value to the team when assigning overall scores to reviews. However, naming other individuals during the meeting is simply inappropriate and unnecessary.

■ *Concentrating on the Money.* Performance appraisals should not center on salary. This is the time to evaluate performance and plan future objectives. Save money discussions for your follow-up meeting where you discuss the overall performance score and its related merit increase.

■ *"Winging It."* Unless you have a plan for what you want to say to the employee, the appraisal will come off as an off-the-cuff discussion of the employee's performance. Know in advance what the most important issues are that you want to discuss with your employee. Make an outline or a list of points you want to cover and refer to it during the session to make sure you don't leave out anything important. Failure to do so could result in the famed "halo and horns" effect, whereby inappropriate generalizations or perceptions of one aspect of a subordinate's performance disproportionately affect your overall view of the individual's capabilities.

■ *Giving Misinformation.* Not wanting to appear less than perfect, supervisors too often make the mistake of providing quick answers to questions whether or not they know the answer. Remember, you'll be seeing the employee again tomorrow, and you can get the answer for her then.

■ *Being Inconsistent.* Again, unless you take the time to plan what you want to stress with the employee and what the final result of the meeting will be, you run the risk of giving inconsistent evaluations and messages. This is not to say that a performance review is either all positive or all negative, but it requires forethought to convey a valuable message.

■ *Toning Down or Avoiding Discussions About Problematic Performance.* More important, without proper preparation, you may fail to discuss problem items openly and honestly during your meeting. As a consequence, you may give an overall score that shows the individual is meeting expectations when indeed she's not. The track record you will have created—that the overall performance for the entire review period was acceptable in the company's eyes—could come back to haunt you later should you attempt to take some kind of adverse action against this worker.

BE PREPARED

The better prepared you are for the performance appraisal, the more productive your discussion will be. The job analysis and performance/work habits review forms (Figure 3-1 on page 20 and 3-2 on page 24 in Chapter 3) will help you to gather your thoughts on the employee's performance and focus in on the areas you want to emphasize. Likewise, if you have been diligent about documenting the employee's performance in a journal, the time to reread your comments is right before the meeting. Just having your journal handy during the meeting is fairly useless unless its contents are fresh in your mind. You don't want to have to start searching through the journal to find documentation on a particular event, so reread this file beforehand and mark the pages that you want to show the employee.

Likewise, remember that performance reviews aren't conducted in a vacuum. It is very important that you first review last year's appraisal to find areas of performance consistency, as well as deviations. This way you'll also be able to see the overall written record that your company is creating and communicating regarding this individual's performance. If an employee were ever to file a lawsuit over a job performance matter, this is exactly what a lawyer would do: Look at current and past performance reviews side by side in an attempt to discern overall trends and patterns. There's no reason you shouldn't do the same.

A common question that arises is, What counts more—a performance review or a written warning in an employee's file? The answer is that it depends on the nature of the written warning.

Whereas *performance*-related infractions are typically subject to steps of progressive discipline (i.e., verbal, written, and final written warnings), many types of *conduct* infractions are not. Stealing, even once, results in summary dismissal—there are no second chances. An incident of insubordination or harassment, on the other hand, may not result in outright dismissal in the company's eyes but could very well result in a final written warning—even for a first-time offense.

That being said, in most arbitrators' and courts' eyes, the annual performance review will carry more weight than a written warning because the performance appraisal represents an entire year's work. The written warning, in contrast, may represent only one bad day in the office. Therefore, if you've dispensed one or more written warnings to a subordinate throughout the performance review period, be sure to document that the employee's overall performance *does not meet expectations*. Otherwise, a positive performance evaluation could nullify the written warnings given during the review period, because you're now documenting that the individual has improved and currently meets overall company expectations.

In addition to getting current on the employee's performance and job responsibilities, you need to anticipate questions or concerns the employee will have about work and about career opportunities within the company. If you have set career objectives with the employee in the past, you should have a written record of them. Locate this list and discern whether the employee has made any strides toward achieving these objectives in the past six to twelve months. If you have changed your mind about the likelihood of the employee being able to reach these goals, formulate in advance what you want to say to the employee on the subject.

TREAT ADULTS LIKE ADULTS

One of the most common reasons supervisors come off appearing awkward or uncomfortable during performance reviews is that they feel obliged to take a paternalistic stance when speaking to the employee.

Remember that your employees are adults, and therefore they have as much right as you do to have their opinions and feelings taken seriously. Consider why you are in the position of supervisor. Chances are it is because you have the most experience and knowledge about your particular field. However, this does not extend to all or any areas outside the workplace. Just because you know the most about phototypesetting or sales or scientific research does not mean you know the most about life or that you can make all the rules regarding behavior.

You may feel that, because you are the supervisor, your employees should automatically follow your career advice. Not so. If you come off being dictatorial, telling your employees what they should do, you are probably only building resentment. But if you hold a discussion in which you and your employee can exchange ideas on an adult-to-adult level, the results may be very rewarding.

Your employees can benefit from your experience, but they will undoubtedly resist doing so unless it is their own choice to make. Therefore, instead of presenting employees with a set agenda to follow, ask questions, elicit opinions and feelings, and invite employees to pick your brain so that together you can make some career decisions that will advance your staff.

The language you use is another factor that affects how you are perceived by your employees. Resorting to clichés or parental-sounding phrases will sometimes alienate people and cause them to believe that you are just spouting jargon instead of relating directly to them as individuals.

Like it or not, the performance appraisal is a time when it is important to get serious. Even if you have a very easygoing relationship with your employees, don't let it spill over into the appraisal interview. At the center of the discussion is the employee's career and livelihood. It's not a time for jokes or idle chat—even if that's what makes both of you more comfortable.

Many employees will spend very little time on their own thinking about what they ultimately want out of their careers. They may not consider how they can improve what they are doing in their present jobs to further those careers. They may not even think through how they are helping to improve productivity so they'll feel justified in requesting more money. It is up to you to insist that all your employees take time during the meeting (actually even before the session starts) to concentrate on how they plan to improve and grow on the job.

Most people feel uncomfortable being serious. It's certainly easier to be funny and make light of things. But take heart; it's not against the rules to smile, be friendly, and make a joke when appropriate. Just make sure that the true purpose of your meeting is accomplished.

CHECKLIST: DON'T START WITHOUT IT

Use this checklist to make sure that you have everything you need handy before you start your performance appraisal:

- ❏ Employee job description
- ❏ Copy of the individual's prior year performance review
- ❏ Employee performance journal or "critical incidents diary"
- ❏ Completed employee self-evaluation forms
- ❏ Record of employee attendance
- ❏ Recent example of employee's work (when appropriate)
- ❏ Examples of work problems you want to discuss
- ❏ List of available training courses appropriate for employee
- ❏ Manual of company policies and rules

CHECKLIST: DO YOU KNOW . . . ?

Go over the following checklist to determine whether you know all you need to about your employees before holding an appraisal meeting. Don't wait until the last minute; give yourself time to find the answers you need.

- ❏ Employee's length of service with company
- ❏ Current projects employee is working on
- ❏ Progress employee is making in current project
- ❏ Employee's educational and experience background
- ❏ Date of employee's last promotion
- ❏ How employee relates to coworkers, clients, and others
- ❏ Level of employee's technical skills

CHAPTER 7

PREPARE YOUR EMPLOYEE

U ntil now, your employees have probably experienced performance appraisals as something that happened *to* them,
something that was *given to* them. Well, no longer. A productive performance appraisal requires the cooperation and collabora-
tion of both the supervisor and the employee. But you can't expect
your employees to be able to jump right in and give themselves
an objective evaluation. You've got to prepare them to be able to
participate in the process.

In Chapter 3, we introduced the job analysis form that should
be filled out by you and also given to each employee. Refer back to
Figure 3-1 on page 20 to recall what types of things are to be en-
tered on the form.

The purpose of the job analysis is for both the employee and
the supervisor to come to an agreement on the major job responsibilities of the position held, and also the relative importance of
each job function. When there is a large difference of opinion here,
it's because there are significant misperceptions between the employee and the supervisor. Going over this form gives you a chance
to straighten out these problems.

Give the employee the form and ask him to list his major job
responsibilities and areas of accountability; the purpose of this ac-

tivity; and the "weight," or amount of time spent and relative importance, of this responsibility within his particular position (totaling 100 percent). Tell him that you will be filling out the same form and that you will then compare what you both have written when the two of you meet three or four days later.

The performance/work habits review should also be completed by both you and the employee. Refer back to Figure 3-2 on page 24 for a copy of this form. Ask the employee to give as honest a self-evaluation as possible. Although it may be hard for employees to assess their own abilities, remind them that the purpose of this form is just to allow you both to get a sense of what areas need work and what skills are the best developed.

SET THINGS STRAIGHT

Just having employees complete a job analysis and performance/ work habits review and setting a convenient date for an appraisal interview are not enough to prepare them. Consider how the following supervisors handled the same situation. Which one of them do you think did a better job?

Supervisor #1: Vicki

Vicki: Hannah, your semiannual performance appraisal is coming up and we're using a new method. I'd like you to take some time to think about your job and how you would rate your own performance. Fill out these two forms and bring them with you when we meet for the appraisal. I've set aside next Tuesday afternoon at 2:00. Is that okay with you?

Hannah: Yes.

Vicki: Fine. Let me know if you have any questions before then.

Supervisor #2: Drew

Drew: Rachel, as you know from the memo I sent out last month, we're going to be handling performance appraisals differently from the way we've done them in the past. I want your input on how you feel you've been doing and also on what you want to be doing in the future. I'm going to ask you to fill out these two forms and bring them with you to our appraisal meeting. Are you free next Tuesday at two?

Rachel: Yes.

Drew: Great. Now, the purpose of the first form is to allow us to come to a consensus on exactly what your job responsibilities are and how you feel about their different priorities and importance. The second form asks you to rate yourself on various job skills and work habits. I know it's hard to judge yourself, but remember, this is not a test and it's not the last word on anything. These forms are meant strictly to identify strong and weak points. I will not be basing any salary increases on what you write here. Also, I guarantee that there will be areas where we disagree. The important thing is that we work together here to come up with a personal improvement program and new job objectives so that you can keep growing and learning.

Rachel: Okay. I understand, Drew.

Drew: Great. Now, I want you to look these forms over and come to me with any questions before you start. Remember, this is still a new process for me, too. We're going to learn it together, okay?

Rachel: Okay. Thanks.

It's really quite obvious which supervisor did the better job in preparing the employee to begin the process of productive performance appraisals. One thing Drew mentioned is an excellent idea for introducing the whole concept of productive performance appraisals to your employees—a memo.

Once you have decided to commit yourself to trying a more productive, collaborative method of conducting performance appraisals, it is very helpful to distribute a memo to your staff members that prepares them for the changes that will be coming soon. Figure 7-1 is an example of such a memo.

FIGURE 7-1. MEMO FOR INTRODUCING NEW PERFORMANCE APPRAISAL PROCEDURES.

Memo: To All Department Members

From: Supervisor

Re: Performance Appraisals

Beginning next month, we will be initiating a new system of performance appraisals in order to make these semiannual meetings more valuable for everyone involved. Before meeting with me for your appraisal, you will receive some self-evaluation forms, which I will ask you to complete and bring to our meeting.

We will also be discussing your job and career objectives, and I ask that you please come to your appraisal meeting prepared to speak on these subjects.

If you have any questions about these forms, please ask me for help right away. I believe that we can make performance appraisals more productive and meaningful, but I will need your cooperation.

Thank you.

SET GOALS

In addition to asking the employee to fill out the job analysis and self-evaluation forms, make sure that your employee knows that you intend to speak about her personal career objectives and that the two of you will work on devising a new action plan together. If you have done this in the past, you might want to provide the employee with a written list of the goals that you both had set during the last review and ask the employee to think about what progress has been made toward those goals, what goals she would like to change, or where she would adjust the priorities that have been set.

Unfortunately, many people feel resentful about being asked to set new objectives for their job performance. "What's wrong with the job I'm doing now?" they ask. "Why do I have to change?"

The honest answer here is that people *do* need to change, because growth on the job keeps it interesting and helps both the employee and the department to work more efficiently. What you have to get across is that you are not asking your employees to set new objectives in order to punish or reprimand them for not performing well. The reasons for setting new objectives are to ensure that employees will continue to feel a sense of achievement and satisfaction in the work they do, to allow them to continue to work toward higher-salaried positions, and for them to be able to increase their value to the company and in the outside job market.

3

COMMON PROBLEMS AND EFFECTIVE SOLUTIONS

CHAPTER 8

WHEN YOU DISAGREE ON ROLES AND GOALS

More often than you'd think, employees and supervisors have entirely different perceptions of the employee's job responsibilities. The longer these misunderstandings go on, the greater the damage to the employee's morale and, ultimately, to the well-being of the department. The job analysis form that has figured so prominently in this book (see Figure 3-1 on page 20 in Chapter 3) has been designed to pinpoint and eliminate these very problems. But first, let's look at some of the reasons why this type of disparity exists in the workplace.

TITLES—A MATTER OF SEMANTICS

What happens when employees are hired or promoted? They are given a job title, right? But with that title often come beliefs and definitions that vary according to the person using it. Consider some of the many "title" words that abound in the workplace— assistant, associate, manager, administrator, senior, junior, trainee, vice president, analyst, partner, junior partner, director, researcher, assistant manager—and these are just the very general terms. Within each profession and business there exist more delineations that may more closely define the person's functions yet still leave many details to the imagination.

PRECEDENCE—IS IT SET IN STONE?

Another determining factor in what is considered to be part of someone's job is invariably what that person's predecessor accomplished. If Rose, as associate bookkeeper, was always responsible for payroll and taxes, does this mean that every subsequent associate bookkeeper is responsible for these tasks? That may depend on how you choose to handle it.

Following precedence is an easy trap to fall into. It follows that time-honored adage, "If it's not broke, don't fix it." But sometimes the simplest way is not the best. The sharp supervisor will realize that each employee newly hired or promoted opens up the opportunity to revise and refine the inner workings of the department. If you are bound to follow whatever came before you, when do you make the time for improvement?

Precedence can also play an unfair part when you are guiding employees in setting career goals. Do you find yourself automatically showing an employee how to take the same steps up the job ladder that her predecessor did? If you are committed to having a productive meeting, you must disregard such temptation and collaborate with each employee on an individual basis without preconceived ideas. Even if the end results have been the same for the last three employees who held that position, it is your job to give that fourth, fifth, or sixth employee the benefit of the doubt and plan for his future based on his individual needs, desires, and abilities.

DISAGREEMENTS ON THE JOB DESCRIPTION

It is precisely because employees and supervisors often disagree on the exact roles of the employee that we recommend these roles be established at the onset of the performance appraisal. If you and the employee don't come to a mutual understanding of what the employee is responsible for and the relative importance of each task and skill, it is impossible to hold a cohesive discussion.

Be sure to have the employee's job description on hand when discussing any disagreement over that employee's responsibilities. The job description can often solve minor problems that tend to be misunderstandings over what is expected of the employee. However, in a productive performance appraisal, you should be prepared to reevaluate the employee's job at each appraisal and be open to amending the written description to more accurately reflect the employee's position. Of course, if your company has no job description on file at the time of the performance review, use this opportunity to work with your employee to create one.

When you review the job analysis form with your employee, you will find that there are two types of discrepancies. Either you and the employee have a significant difference of opinion about the fundamental purpose of the position, or you disagree about specific tasks and whether they are actually an integral part of the employee's job. Let's first examine the more serious situation—disagreeing about the fundamental role of the employee in the department.

Suppose your employee has the title of assistant researcher. You believe her major job function is to support and assist the staff's senior researchers. However, it is clear from the employee's performance, and from the job analysis form, that the employee believes the most important part of her job is the independent, smaller research projects she is also given to work on. What should you focus on in this situation?

First, recognize why there is the difference of opinion between you and your employee. In this instance, you may each have a separate agenda. You, as the supervisor, view an assistant researcher as skilled support staff whose job it is to make the work of the more senior staff members easier and more productive. The employee, however, if she is ambitious, sees the position as a temporary one that will lead to a more senior position in due course. Therefore, the employee is more interested in completing independent assignments that allow her to prove her ability to succeed.

Certainly, both of your opinions are understandable. But it is up to you, as manager, to blend the two of them into an agreeable arrangement. Use what the employee has written in the job analysis form to clarify what she believes is the more important function of her job. Then state what you need from her in terms of support services and the reasons she is needed there. Is the employee concerned that you will not be open to promoting her after she has proven herself ready? Discuss the circumstances and assure her that she can be judged by the support she gives senior members as well as by the independent projects she does.

AGREEMENTS ON THE JOB DESCRIPTION

If your employee is very insistent about wanting to work on independent projects, it may be best to be open to the suggestion and make arrangements for the employee to be given the opportunity. You do, however, have the right to explain that he may have to wait some time for promotion and that it cannot be an automatic event that occurs after a predetermined amount of time.

Disagreeing about the responsibility for specific tasks can also cause a temporary obstacle in conducting your appraisal. Too often, employees resent being asked to do things they believe are not part of their job. Once these feelings are brought out into the open, you can settle these matters and repair any damage that may have been done.

Before getting on the defensive, take the time to determine if an employee's resentment toward any specific task is justified. Why is the employee complaining? Do coworkers at the same level have the same responsibility, or is this employee singled out? Is there a question of an employee being asked to perform a specific task based on gender? This can be a particularly sensitive issue and such assignments should be avoided. Does the employee feel he is being held back professionally because of required tasks that may not reflect the progress he has made? All of these possibilities need to be considered before taking a stand.

If you've decided that regardless of the employee's feelings the task in question is legitimately part of his job, take a firm but dispassionate stand. When personalities get involved, supervisors are tempted to throw their weight around, but that will only create permanent rifts in the employee-supervisor relationship. Explain your position matter-of-factly and request that the employee cooperate and continue to be responsible for the task. Don't make a big issue out of "winning" here. Go on to the next topic—preferably one you are in agreement about—as quickly as you can.

CLASHING ON GOALS

Chapter 3 presented an example of an employee and a supervisor in agreement over performance goals to set for the employee. But what happens when that is not the case? What do you do when an employee has ideas about goals that you believe are very unrealistic, or does not agree that improvement is necessary?

Before you answer this question, keep in mind that no matter how certain you may be about something, the employee also has a right to an opinion. You should try to guide your employees, and you can set standards of performance that must be met. However, unless you can convince the employee to buy in to your plan, performance will suffer.

Let's look at one example of how to handle this situation. Barbara is in a junior analyst's position in a financial-planning firm that caters to middle-income clients. She is mainly involved in researching investments and analyzing portfolios to help her manager, Al, and senior staff members prepare recommendations for their clients.

Al: Barbara, tell me, have you given much thought to how you think you can improve your job performance? I'd like us to work on setting some goals for you so that we can make sure you're getting the experience and training you need for the future as well as for the job you're doing now.

Barbara: I feel that I'm very competent at my job. The only problem I see is that I don't get enough of an opportunity to take on greater responsibility. I'd like to work with clients more than I've been doing rather than just focusing on back-end research.

Al: Really? I'm surprised to hear that. I was under the impression that you're still not fully comfortable dealing directly with clients. I assumed that you would feel that you would need to be surer of your abilities and more fluent in the marketplace before you take charge of a project.

Wisely, Al is cautious about sounding too critical of her ideas. He wants to hear more of Barbara's thoughts before forming an opinion.

Barbara: Oh, I've been doing a lot of work on my own to prepare myself to work with clients. Actually, I've given it some serious thought, and it seems that if you want to make money, you've got to be the one who handles it. I'm ready to show our clients how to handle their money.

Al: That's an interesting theory. I know that you have your basic financial certifications, but I don't recall that you took many finance courses in school. Am I right?

Barbara: That's true. But real-world experience counts for something, doesn't it? And my certifications may be recent, but they're still valid. Besides, I've learned so much since I started working here.

Al: Yes. But I feel you still have a lot to learn. Our business is too risky to learn as you go, since it involves other people's money. You need to continue researching investments and analyzing client portfolios under close supervision before you take on that responsibility.

Barbara: Well, sure, but when do I get to make some decisions? How will we know when I *am* ready?

Al: That's a good question. I think what you're really telling me is that you're a little impatient to move ahead with your career. I can appreciate that. I'm going to ask you to continue learning through experience for three more months. At that time, if you and I feel you are ready, I will assign you to work with a senior staff member on a client portfolio in which you will be able to make internal suggestions. Then you and I, and the senior staffer, will go over your choices together to evaluate if they would be in the client's best interests.

Barbara: But I want to get involved in working directly with the clients. Can I start on that, at least?

Al: You certainly have a lot of ambition. Slow down. Client contact is a very delicate matter. It's quite easy to scare off a client by being too aggressive or just saying the wrong thing. Let's arrange for you to begin quietly sitting in on advisory sessions in three months, okay? Temper your ambitions slightly and master the research and analysis responsibilities you've got now. We'll do our best to expose you to client development in due time.

Barbara: Well, I guess that makes sense. But I still feel that I'm more ready than you think.

Al: I appreciate your frustration, but you're going to have to go along with me on this. If I let you do something that I didn't believe you are capable of, I wouldn't be doing either of us any favors. Now, do I have your commitment that you will continue to work on these skills over the next three months?

By keeping his cool and hearing what Barbara was *really* saying, Al was able to avoid putting her on the defensive by coming out and criticizing her plan. Although he has doubts about her present abilities, he is willing to be more aggressive in training her to take on more responsibility, since she obviously has the desire. However, Al is careful to maintain control over the situation. He makes it clear that she will not be given any more autonomy until he is absolutely convinced that he is being fair to a client by placing the client in Barbara's hands. Barbara may not ascend her career ladder as quickly as she would like, but Al is going to make sure that she's ready for whatever she takes on.

Helping employees choose goals that are most appropriate for them is basically a matter of listening and asking the right questions. You can use this list of dos and don'ts as a guide:

DO: Ask employees to fully explain their career plans and their reasoning before offering an opinion.

DO: Repeat what the employee tells you about his goals, especially if you may not agree with them, so that the employee can hear what it sounds like aloud. This simple technique can actually make a difference.

DO: Help employees choose goals that you will be comfortable helping them achieve. When personal goals clash with what is best for the department, offer alternatives that can satisfy both parties.

DON'T: Offer your own plan for success to the employee. Collaborate together, and let the employee formulate most of the ideas. The employee will be more committed to a plan that he has devised himself.

DON'T: Be afraid to give your opinion when asked. Be aware, though, of any prejudices you may have, and remember that even though something may not be right for you, it could be right for the employee.

DON'T: Be judgmental if an employee chooses to take a path different from your own. Be objective and consider only whether the goals are in the best interest of the employee and the department.

ASKING THE RIGHT QUESTIONS

The best way to get someone to change his mind to your way of thinking is to get him to come to that conclusion on his own. When employees choose inappropriate goals, or if they have trouble planning for the future, you can help them by asking the right questions to get their minds going in the right direction. Here are some questions you may be able to use in your own discussions with your employees. Add questions of your own to this list—particularly questions that deal implicitly with your organization or line of business.

Questions About Goals

■ What do you see as your next move in career progression? How do you think you can best work toward reaching that goal? What type of time frame would you see yourself committing to?

■ Are you interested in taking any outside courses? Would you be interested in attending training seminars available through the company?

■ What long-range goals would you set for yourself? How are you working toward reaching those goals now? What do you plan for the future?

■ How is your present job preparing you for the goals you are setting? Is your present job setting the right foundation, or is there another path that you might consider that might be easier to pursue?

■ What do you know about the requirements for the goals you have set for yourself? Do you need to find out more?

■ Where do you think you would end up, ultimately, if you did not actively seek to change your career course? What would be the pros and cons of such circumstances?

■ What career changes will you have to make to reach the goals you are setting? Can they be made within the boundaries of your present position?

CHAPTER 9

WHEN THE NEWS IS BAD

G iving a performance appraisal to a poor performer is one of the more unpleasant tasks of being a supervisor, but like it or not, it's part of the job. How would you deal with this situation?

Pamela: We both know that there have been problems with your performance. Although we've discussed what's wrong on several occasions, let's use this time to see if we can clarify where your performance needs improvement.

William: But I *have* been trying. Do you mean that I can't get a satisfactory rating this time?

Pamela: Yes. I wish I could tell you otherwise. We have to have a consistent record on file documenting a number of the problems we've experienced throughout the year—that's only fair. I believe that this does not come as a surprise to you.

William: Well, not really.

Pamela: William, I'd like to give you another chance. Let's not dwell on the past except to identify the problems and see how we can correct them. Although this performance review will indeed reflect problems we've experienced with your performance, from today on, we have a fresh goal to reach. Starting today, you are going to improve your work performance. In the not-too-distant future, I want to be able to share good news with you when we meet for your interim performance review. How does that sound?

William: That sounds fair.

Pamela: Fine. Now, have you filled out the forms I've given you? Let's see where we are in agreement and where we are not.

The good news is that a productive appraisal, even with a substandard overall score, can be an effective tool for turning around that employee's behavior. In this case, Pamela confronts William head-on with news he already knows—that his general rating of performance is unsatisfactory. But rather than spend time berating William for the past, Pamela suggests that they use the appraisal to correct William's problem performance. She also makes sure to give William a consistent message that his performance must improve if he wants to remain with the company.

Fortunately, Pamela has been doing her job well all along. Instead of waiting until his review, Pamela and William have already discussed the problems with his performance, and she has made him aware that unless he improves there will be consequences to pay. But like many people, William seems to need the lesson of a poor performance rating before he takes the situation as seriously as he should.

Although William may have chosen to ignore his unsatisfactory performance until now, at this point he seems ready to admit the problem and work toward changing the situation. This is primarily because he was expecting to hear what Pamela had to say. From this point on, Pamela can follow the same pattern she would with any other performance appraisal, discussing how to improve performance, set productivity goals, and plan for the future.

GUIDELINES FOR AN APPRAISAL WITH A POOR PERFORMER

Many times employees will deny that they are not performing up to the standards set for the department. If you are not prepared, you can spend a lot of time just arguing the point of whether the employee is truly underperforming. When you are faced with this type of employee, turn to the following guidelines to keep the meeting productive:

■ *Have documentation available.* Mark entries in the employee journal with paper clips so that you can quickly show examples of problems the employee has had with performance and/or behavior over the past six months. Remember that substandard work product shared with the employee at the time of occurrence makes for a solid record of evidence. You have every right to revisit these samples during the annual performance review since it reflects the entire year's performance.

■ *Make sure you have also documented the times you have spoken to the employee about job performance.* This effort should put an end to any insisting by employees that they were unaware any problem existed. In fact, it is typically a good idea to incorporate dates, times, and results of discussions held regarding substandard job performance right into the performance appraisal narrative.

■ *Have written quality standards to show to the employee.* These standards should be distributed to all employees at hiring or when a promotion is given.

■ *Prepare a list of changes you would like the employee to make in performance.* Don't just say, "You have to improve." Be specific on exactly what needs to change and how. Give specific examples, using the "by . . ." format, like this:

I expect you to improve your overall customer service performance *by following up* with internal customers within two hours of their initial calls, *by meeting them* in their offices rather than asking them to come to yours, and *by maintaining* weekly contact regarding the status of open claims.

■ *Be positive about the employee's ability to improve.* If appropriate, arrange for extra training or closer supervision by yourself or a senior coworker. Present this idea to the employee not as a punishment, but as a solution to the problem. However, be careful not to overpromise in the area of dedicated, one-on-one training. No supervisor can provide one-on-one training forever, and if you document an open-ended promise, your documentation may be used against you should you try to terminate the individual for substandard job performance at a later date.

Therefore, use limiting comments like, "I will work with you every Monday morning from 9:00 to 9:30 A.M. in my office *for the next three weeks* to ensure that you are processing incoming claims efficiently." Such language documents your company's proactive and rehabilitative efforts at helping the worker meet performance goals. However, if you do not limit your commitment to three weeks, or worse, if you document that you will provide training and then fail to do so, your actions may be interpreted as insincere. A plaintiff attorney may then argue that you set up the employee to fail and that your company's termination decision should be reversed.

■ *Set new short- and long-term goals for the employee.* Long-term goals give the discussion a positive feeling, but tell the employee that for now he should concentrate on the short-term goals and that when improvement is made you will meet again to create a plan on how to obtain future goals.

■ *Be honest with your employees about their future without being patronizing or admonishing.* Spell out exactly what employees have to do to improve and what the consequences will be if they cannot change their performance. If an employee's job is in jeopardy, say so, not as a threat but as a factual observation. Not only is this fair to the employee, but it is essential to protecting yourself and your company in any legal actions a discharged employee may file in the future.

In fact, many supervisors provide workers with substandard performance reviews (i.e., the overall score shows the individual fails to meet expectations) but feel they must wait thirty or sixty days to provide a written warning. That isn't necessarily the case. Under certain circumstances, you have the right to turn the substandard performance review into a written warning by employing language like this:

> In addition to documenting that your overall performance for this review period does not meet company expectations, this annual appraisal serves as a formal written warning. Failure to demonstrate immediate and sustained improvement may result in further disciplinary action, up to and including dismissal.

You'll thereby create a written record that the individual's employment is in serious jeopardy of being lost at this point. Note, though, that this action may seem a bit extreme, depending on your company's past practices, and a collective-bargaining agreement may preclude such a "combined step." Still, depending on the nature of the infraction, and the individual's tenure with your company and status as a protected worker, it could be worth pursuing. When in doubt, check with your company's human resources department or qualified outside counsel regarding your rights as an employer to combine written warnings with annual performance appraisals.

■ *Make an agreement with the employee to improve performance within a certain amount of time.* Set measurable standards for the improvement and plan together exactly how it can be accomplished. Agree to meet again in one to three months to assess the progress that has been made. Remember as well that you have the discretion to delay the formal performance appraisal and merit increase decision for thirty, sixty, or ninety days. You can certainly revisit overall performance at that point and, if successful, provide your employee with a higher score than she would have received had you stuck to the "formal" reviewing cycle. Be sure to note the reason for the delay in the narrative description of the review, however, just so that the appropriate record is made.

A QUESTION OF "ATTITUDE"

Sometimes we think an employee is a poor performer, but when we sit down and try to rate his performance, we find that his skills and abilities are more than adequate. Instead, we realize that the problem is a question of "attitude," although you'll want to be sure to avoid the word *attitude* in any of your discussions with the individual and especially in any of your documentation. (Use terms like *conduct* and *behavior* instead.)

Some attitude problems do actual damage to performance. For example, if an employee displays a surly attitude when interacting with customers, it certainly can adversely affect business. In contrast, arriving late to the office, being inconsiderate of others, or being careless with company property may not directly affect the employee's work, but these behaviors are probably disruptive to the rest of the department and can definitely damage the morale of the employee's coworkers.

Discussing an attitude problem with an employee is probably a more uncomfortable situation than citing inadequate performance. It puts you in the awkward position of acting like a parent reprimanding a child when you should be able to deal with each of your employees on an adult level. Still, *conduct* infractions are separate from *performance* transgressions, and in many ways they are more disruptive and damaging.

You can get past this dilemma by refusing to treat the employee like a child and stating the problem without voicing any judgments about it. The following guidelines can help you plan what to say:

Dos and Don'ts in Discussing Attitude Problems

Don't Say	*Do Say*
Your personality is too abrasive to your coworkers and to me.	You need to speak more respectfully to both your coworkers and your supervisors.

I don't like your attitude.	Your behavior shows that you seem to resent doing the work that is asked of you. If that is not true, you need to change the perception you're creating in terms of your willingness to assume your rightful responsibilities. (Cite specific examples.)
It's too bad you'll never succeed with your attitude.	You have the ability to do well and succeed. You need to change the behaviors that are standing in the way of your success.

The term *attitude* is a very subjective judgment that courts of law will often dismiss because it is associated with a mere difference of opinion or personality conflict. In addition, the word itself connotes feelings of patronization and condescension. Therefore, be sure to describe objective behaviors that create a negative perception of the employee in the eyes of other people. Only behaviors and actions that can be observed and documented may be presented as evidence in court.

The truth is, you and the employee will both know that it is the employee's attitude you are discussing, but if you keep the emphasis on specific behaviors *you have documented,* you eliminate the opportunity for the employee to say that you are "picking on him," "misinterpreting his actions," or holding him to a higher standard than everyone else in the group.

DEALING WITH EMOTIONAL OUTBURSTS

Occasionally, some employees will have such unrealistic expectations or perceptions of their role that they will react very strongly if disappointed with the performance review that is given. This situation can unnerve even the most experienced manager. Crying, clamming up, and shouting are all reactions that can be very difficult to deal with. Here are some suggestions for getting through such a situation:

■ *Crying.* An employee in tears is probably not able to discuss things calmly. Try to minimize the employee's embarrassment by not becoming agitated. Offer compassion and a box of tissues. Ask the employee if she would like to talk a little later, or give the employee time to compose herself by leaving the room for a while.

■ *Clamming Up.* An employee who is feeling a lot of hostility or resentment toward you may react by avoiding talking to you altogether. Here, again, you need to be the more mature person. Talk to the employee about whatever you need to, but don't push the issue by attempting to make small talk. It is best not to make too big a deal out of the incident, because chances are it will pass before too long. If, however, the situation continues, you will have to address the employee directly and request that he talk to you so that you can put the problem behind you.

■ *Shouting.* Don't answer shouting with more shouting. Instead, talk calmly, slowly, and firmly to the employee and do not appear frightened. If the shouting continues without abatement, ask the employee to leave. Such gross insubordination may typically result in immediate dismissal in and of itself. If you feel threatened physically, by all means call security for assistance. You reserve the discretion to terminate the individual, by phone, once he is off your premises. However, you will make a better record for your company if you place the individual on a paid investigatory leave at that point, have a third party such as HR conduct an objective and timely investigation, and reserve your decision until a reasonable conclusion can be reached.

THE IMPORTANCE OF FOLLOW-UP

Although follow-up is important with all employees, it is even more crucial when dealing with a poor performer. Such employees have been dealt a blow to their egos—to their self-confidence—and they need continual guidance and reassurance that they can succeed on the job.

Once you have identified the problem and charted a course for the employee to follow, don't look to continually find fault with the employee's work—you made your point at the performance appraisal. If you are satisfied that the employee's motivation is real, try to point out what he is doing right and encourage him to keep it up. You needn't keep reminding the employee of his past failures. If you have counseled the employee well, it is now time to accentuate the positive.

The problem most supervisors have with giving poor performance reviews is that they feel a need to keep talking in order to justify their opinion. Instead, you need to take the attitude that you are going to work with the employee to plan how to improve performance without being judgmental over "why" there exists such a need for change. Treat employees like the adults they are, and if they are truly willing to work hard, you are likely to be happy with the results. In short, get over it and move on.

CHAPTER 10

WATCH OUT FOR PITFALLS

"**A** beautiful woman like you can go very far in this company if you make the right connections."

Who said that? Was it you? Let's hope not.

No matter how innocent or even flattering you may mean a remark to be, commenting on an employee's appearance is absolutely forbidden during a performance appraisal (and is almost always out of line at other times, too). Sexual harassment has become such a sensitive issue in today's workplace that supervisors need to be extra careful not to say anything that could be interpreted as suggestive or threatening. It may be second nature or well meaning for you to comment on a woman's new hairstyle or clothing, but it has no place in a performance review.

If it is your practice to begin the meeting on a complimentary note, compliment *the work* your employee has done recently. Beginning an appraisal meeting by saying "You're looking great today" is not acceptable office etiquette. Likewise, be sure to avoid diminutive terms like honey, sweetie, and dear in any of your business conversations. Such off-the-cuff comments appear demeaning and condescending and add zero value to your workplace interpersonal relationships. In fact, they are often cited as primary evidence of a manager's lack of sensitivity to others.

This is not exclusively a man/woman issue, either. Women are also being accused of harassing men, and anyone can be subject to accusations of homosexual harassment.

Does this advice make you afraid to open your mouth? It really shouldn't. It is just very important that you think before you speak and that you keep all discussion during performance appraisals on a professional level.

Sexual innuendo is just one of the pitfalls that can trap supervisors if they aren't careful. As noted, remarks that can be construed as sexually or romantically suggestive are dangerous, but other types of personal remarks can also get you into trouble. Let's go over some of the more common and most dangerous ones so that you can avoid making any serious mistakes.

KEEP IT STRICTLY BUSINESS

Religion and politics have traditionally been sensitive subjects of conversation in social settings. If you bring up these topics in the office, you are playing with fire. Don't ask employees what they think of an upcoming election as an icebreaker during your performance appraisal meeting, and refrain from asking any questions about religious holidays—especially if they differ from your own.

Even seemingly neutral topics such as real estate or vacations do not belong in the appraisal interview. The reason these topics are objectionable is that if you ask certain types of questions, it can be interpreted as actually seeking information about the employee's finances—something that is not your business. You can inquire about the well-being of an employee's family, but don't get into a discussion on family planning or size, lest you be accused of being prejudiced against employees who seek to expand their families and further "burden" the company with medical insurance premiums and maternity leave.

Another hazardous situation to watch out for is when the discussion begins to include other people in the office. Although you may think the employee will keep whatever you say in confidence (after all, he said he would never repeat anything you discuss), don't take the chance. Office politics is too tempting a subject for gossip, and anything the manager says about anyone else is really too good for employees to keep to themselves.

If an employee tries to get you to explain why you did this or that for another coworker, or why another person deserved that promotion when he was passed over for the job, don't fall into the trap. Bring the subject back to the employee himself and speak about why you've taken actions (or lack of actions) on the part of the employee based on his performance, experience, and knowledge. Even though one employee will try to compare himself to another employee, that does not mean you must justify your decisions based on this premise. Say something like, "Let's talk about you, not her," and bring the discussion back to where you want it to be.

Small talk aside, you can still get into real trouble if you're not careful what you say, even when you do stick to business. The biggest pitfall you can fall prey to is making a promise to an employee that you are unable to keep. No matter how casually you may think your promise was made, we guarantee that your employee will take it as seriously as an oath written in blood. Therefore, be sure to think twice, and then once again, when promising an employee any of the following:

- Money
- A promotion
- Training programs
- Improved assignments
- An upgrade or change of office or work space
- New equipment

We aren't suggesting that you cannot commit yourself to anything, only warning you that you must be sure of your ability to make good on any promise that you make. You can promise to *try* to do something for your employee during a performance appraisal, but make it very clear that you do not know if you can succeed and that the employee should not count on anything until you are able to find out for certain.

DON'T TALK DOLLARS

Although the most pressing detail every employee will want to know is, "How much of a raise can I get?" we advise that you keep money out of the appraisal process until the follow-up meeting, discussed in Chapter 11.

A productive performance appraisal must focus entirely on the employee's performance—the identification of strengths and weaknesses, and the development of new goals and objectives for the near and far terms. Once money enters the discussion, interest in talking about how the employee can improve will quickly dissipate.

When an employee inevitably brings up the subject of money, state that you will discuss it at a later time; for now, you want to concentrate only on performance. If the employee insists, you can further explain that you do not make the final decision about money and that you will make your recommendation based in large part on the outcome of the current meeting.

Let your employees know that, like it or not, you can exert a much greater influence on how they achieve their personal career goals than on the exact salary they receive. With some exceptions, salary increases generally have to meet certain company guidelines, and there is not a great deal of flexibility to work with.

THE TROUBLE ZONES

Watching out for pitfalls requires more than just making sure you don't bring up the wrong subject. You are just as likely to say the wrong thing in response to a question or a statement made by an employee.

It can happen to the most careful manager. You may know ex-

actly what to say and what not to say, and yet an employee may
bring up a subject that can get you into a lot of trouble if you give
the wrong answer. How good are you at avoiding these trouble
zones? To see if you recognize a pitfall in time, take the following
exercise. We've answered the first two questions and left the rest
for you to respond to.

EXERCISE: AVOIDING TROUBLE ZONES

Question

"Why did Adeline get promoted last month when I've been here two months longer than
her and I'm still waiting?"

Sample Answer

"It was not a choice between the two of you. Let's stick to talking about you. I'm sorry,
but I don't think you're ready for promotion just yet, and I'll explain why."

Question

"Gee, that's a nice new suit. You look great. Have you been working out or something?"

Sample Answer

"Thank you. Now, getting back to business . . ."

Question

"I'm really interested in that new training program for secretaries, but I heard you have to
get recommendations from three managers. Could you get me into the program?"

Your Answer

_____

_____

_____

_____

Question

"My last supervisor promised me a big raise at my next review. Now that I've been trans-
ferred to your department, will that still be true?"

Your Answer

_____

_____

_____

_____

Question

"I used to enjoy working with Andy, but lately he's been difficult to deal with. I think he's been drinking again. What do you think?"

Your Answer

_____

_____

_____

_____

Question

"I really need to get a promotion soon. You know what it's like, being a single parent yourself. There's just never enough to go around."

Your Answer

_____

_____

_____

_____

Question

"What are you going to do about filling Tina's spot if she doesn't come back after her maternity leave? I'm next in line, right?"

Your Answer

_____

_____

_____

_____

PART IV

WRAPPING IT UP

CHAPTER 11

THE POST-APPRAISAL MEETING

You've made it through the session; you've dodged the pitfalls and managed to honestly communicate with your employee. Together, the two of you have established some new short-term objectives and have refined the long-term career goals to suit new interests and new perceptions of opportunity. You're ready to close the books on this performance appraisal, aren't you?

Sorry, not so fast. You must still hold a final "post mortem" meeting to discuss salary and upcoming plans for new assignments, training, changed behavior, improved performance, and anything else that surfaced during the interview. It is in this meeting that the employee receives a final rating (i.e., the Overall Score) and learns of the merit increase amount.

In addition, you should share the financial review with your employee in advance of this final meeting. This way, he'll have a chance to review your final comments in light of his self-evaluation and your actual discussions during the performance appraisal interview. This is, after all, the document that will make its way into the employee's permanent record, so the more time he has to study it in advance, the better. Let's go back to see how Harvey and his employee, Matthew, from Chapter 3 did.

Harvey: I believe we covered quite a lot in your performance review the other day, Matthew. Although I was mainly pleased with your performance before, I think we've worked through the few trouble spots we have. I want to congratulate you and let you know that your overall rating for this review period is a 4. I'm happy to tell you that your overall merit increase for the upcoming year will be 4 percent. You can see on this form how I arrived at your overall score, and the merit increase will become effective in the next payroll period. For now, let's go over the list of goals we set last week and talk about anything else you'd like to do that would help you meet these goals—something perhaps we didn't think of already. Otherwise, I think we can happily conclude this review and get to work on making many of the things we've discussed happen.

Matthew: Okay. Thanks, Harvey. This was an interesting process.

Harvey: Thank you for your cooperation. You've made it an interesting process for me as well.

Harvey does a good job in ending the performance appraisal interview. Notice how he uses "we" instead of "you" when he talks to Matthew about improving performance and reaching new goals. By doing so he shares in the responsibility of making these improvements—something responsible managers should be doing.

Harvey has done a good amount of work since his initial meeting with Matthew. First, he completed the overall review form, taking Matthew's self-assessment and discussions during the actual review into consideration. He then submitted his finalized review to his own boss and to human resources for final approval. He returned the finalized review to Matthew in advance of their post-appraisal meeting so that Matthew would have time to carefully and objectively review it. The postmortem then gave Harvey the chance to communicate Matthew's overall performance score and merit increase amount and to follow up regarding any pending items or suggestions. The end result was a fair and objective assessment of Matthew's performance throughout the review period, a realistic and workable development plan, and an employee who had the opportunity "to be heard" during the entire process. Now that's empowerment and leadership in action!

A SUMMARY OF THE PROCESS

One of the challenges that many managers face lies in gaining a clearer understanding of the time line surrounding the performance appraisal process. Here's a short outline with suggestions on when to communicate your expectations and set up the actual appraisal meeting(s). Keep in mind, though, that this is definitely a flexible structure and should be adapted to fit your personal management style.

THE PRODUCTIVE APPRAISAL TIME LINE

Step 1: One month before appraisals are formally due . . .

Prepare your employees in advance of your intention to reinvent the way that your company currently conducts performance appraisals by issuing a short memo (see Figure 7-1 on page 65). Confirm that the revised goal will be to make the process more collaborative by asking employees for greater input in terms of their performance assessments and career development plans.

Step 2: Two weeks before appraisal meetings are to occur . . .

Provide your subordinates with either (1) a copy of their current job descriptions or (2) a job analysis form (see Figure 3-1 on page 20) as well as a copy of last year's review. Ask them to review and/or document their primary versus secondary job responsibilities and rank them in terms of importance. Request that they "weight" each activity so that all responsibilities total 100 percent. This way you can establish a baseline agreement for what's being evaluated or discuss your differences in perception regarding the individual's key roles and responsibilities.

Likewise, ask employees to complete a performance/work habits review form (see Figure 3-2 on page 24), also known as a self-evaluation, using the three critical questions on pages 13 and 14 to help them objectively identify their strengths and weaknesses as well as ideas for their future training and career-development needs.

Step 3: One week before you're required to complete the individual's formal evaluation . . .

Review the employee's self-evaluation forms with her in a one-on-one meeting. Do you agree with the weightings that she assigned to her key responsibilities on the job analysis form or job description? Can you identify any major discrepancies? Next, ask her to review her self-evaluation and career development plan with you. Listen attentively and then gently discuss suggestions or alternatives. Remember, this initial meeting allows the employee to be heard and requires you to listen. Very little advance preparation is due on your part for this meeting.

Step 4: On the day of the actual performance review . . .

Meet with your employee and provide your own formal feedback regarding strengths, areas for development, and the nature of the development plan that she outlined. (It is highly recommended that you have your human resources or legal departments review any formal performance appraisals before they are given to the employee, especially if the individual is on some kind of performance improvement plan or other disciplinary status.) Make sure to emphasize that you've considered all of her feedback and suggestions in creating this annual performance review. Talk openly and candidly about discrepancies in your respective perceptions with the intent of coming to an agreement on where to go from here.

Note: You'll see that this suggested review format actually entails two meetings with each of your direct reports: one in which you listen (Step 3) and one in which you talk (Step 4). You can combine both of these steps into one meeting, if you like. However, all the work that's gone on prior to this one-on-one formal review meeting here in Step 4 was done by the candidate, not by you. Therefore, you'll have delegated the responsibility for self-evaluation and future career development planning to the employee, placing you in the role of career mentor and coach rather than unilateral disciplinarian and decision maker. Such are the makings of brilliant leaders!

Step 5: Three to five days after the formal performance review is held and your written appraisal has been given to the employee . . .

Conduct a follow-up meeting for two reasons: (1) to confirm agreement on the overall review, new projects and responsibilities, and long-term career development plans; and (2) to inform the individual of the merit increase amount associated with the overall performance score listed at the very end of the performance review. Ask for additional suggestions to make the department work more efficiently and effectively.

Prepare to conduct informal appraisals at least six (but ideally three) months from now. Let the employee know that you'll ask her to review her then-current responsibilities, progression in terms of her short-term goals and projects, and even longer-term career development plans (if they have changed).

Again, emphasize that you prefer to have interim reviews throughout the (annual) review period so that you can both assess progress, but that you expect your subordinates to take the lead in gathering data and making the appropriate assessments. Such "sharing" allows staff members to motivate themselves and reinvent themselves in light of your company's changing needs. And little does more to build a shared sense of openness, a greater sense of partnership, and increased accountability than these intermittent opportunities to focus on your staff member's specific needs and accomplishments.

That's what people development and great leadership are all about.

YOUR RIGHTS AND RESPONSIBILITIES AS A SUPERVISOR

Although we have stressed the collaborative aspect of a productive performance appraisal, this doesn't allow you to abdicate making a judgment on the final rating of the employee's performance. This appraisal form is important for informational purposes so that the employee can understand how the rating, compensation, and promotion systems operate.

If your future plans for the employee include a new type of training, try to have as much information as possible about the program he will be entering. If you can give an exact date, or at least indicate the month it will be in, you will have given the employee something very concrete to anticipate.

If you and the employee have set precise goals for promotion, it is wise to once again go over exactly what requirements must be met before a promotion can be granted. If promotions cannot be given unless a specific opening exists, this requirement must be made very clear to the employee.

THE STATUS QUO

As often as not, the end result of a performance review will be that an employee's job will not have any substantial changes, so you are actually encouraging the individual to maintain the status quo. This presents a special challenge during the post-appraisal interview, because you may not have any entirely new goals to cheer the employee on to accomplishing.

When this is the case, turn the meeting into another opportunity to express your appreciation for the dependable, consistent good work that the employee has been doing. Reiterate that you want the employee to gain more experience and knowledge and to continue to be a valuable member of the department.

With all employees, use the post-appraisal interview to again emphasize your interest in the employee's personal and career growth by offering your assistance with these goals. Thank the employee for her cooperation in making the performance appraisal a productive work session and express your confidence that she will be able to act on the plans that have been made.

SAVE THE MONEY FOR LAST

We strongly suggest that you wait until the end of the discussion before informing employees about their salary increase. The reason is simple: Once you share the decision, the employee is likely to be very distracted. It's human nature. Once you give a dollar amount, the person will undoubtedly be doing complicated mental calculations, trying to determine if she can now buy that car that's at the top of the list. And you will know immediately whether the employee had been expecting more or less than the amount you have promised.

If you have done your job well up until this point, the amount of money involved should not come as a great surprise at either extreme of the spectrum. If your employee had been expecting a lot more, ask yourself if you either said anything to give him false expectations or failed to make sure he understood the level of satisfaction you have with his performance.

Although the post-appraisal interview is the time to finalize plans and intentions that were brought out during the review, don't feel that it must be the end of the process until six months or a year have passed. The reason that many performance problems continue is that managers neglect the daily reactions and feedback employees need in order to change their behaviors. Check in with your employees regularly to see if progress is being made. If you're not pleased with the results, talk to them seriously about what else can be done. Keep the review process going on a steady basis. After all, a formal performance review may occur only once a year, but ongoing feedback and open communication are the hallmarks of a solid leader. Whether that translates into daily, weekly, or monthly feedback—formal or informal—is up to you. But as a general rule of thumb, you should ideally meet with all of your subordinates, one-on-one, at least quarterly to ensure that you understand how they're performing and, equally as important, they realize that you're watching what they're doing.

AN ISSUE OF MECHANICS

Supervisors often wonder what the "spread" of overall performance scores across a department should look like. Although there's no one uniform answer at any given point in time, performance appraisal consultant Dick Grote recommends the following distribution:

Performance Rating	Percentage of People Who Typically Receive This Rating
5. Outstanding	Less than 5%
4. Exceeds Expectations	About 30%
3. Meets Expectations	About 50%
2. Needs Improvement	About 15%
1. Fails to Meet Expectations/Unsatisfactory	Less than 5%

SOURCE: Dick Grote, *The Performance Appraisal Question and Answer Book* (New York: AMACOM, 2002), p. 164.

Furthermore, there's often a question about the difference between a rating of 2 (Needs Improvement) and 1 (Unsatisfactory). It's best to check with your company to see how it defines those differences and what implications, if any, should follow. Generally speaking, though, an overall score of 2 typically still allows the individual to participate in the merit increase pool. You may only choose to give 1 percent, for example, out of a possible 4 percent, but the individual may receive a merit increase nonetheless. In addition, it is common to find that someone with a score of 2 receives a "performance improvement plan" to raise his overall score to an acceptable level of 3 in the future.

In comparison, a worker who receives an overall score of Unsatisfactory typically may not participate in the merit pool at all. In addition, the performance review may be drafted to include written warning language, as discussed in Chapter 9.

Finally, if 50 percent of employees generally receive an overall performance score of 3, showing that they meet company expectations, why do so many employees interpret that grade as a putdown? And why do so many managers feel guilty handing it out as a final score?

The answer, unfortunately, lies in how we equate a score of 3 as being middle-of-the-road, not in any way outstanding or stellar. To use the grammar-school metaphor, it's like getting a C. However, in the workplace, "meets expectations" is not the equivalent of a C at school. In fact, it's much more than that. It indicates that the employee is fully successful in the role, demonstrating the appropriate level of mastery, time commitment, and the like. "Superior" and "distinguished" performance, by contrast, can typically only occur when someone not only performs at a fully successful level but clearly stands out as a rarity among his peers for any number of reasons, not the least of which is a track record of outstanding achievements and accomplishments that can be quantified and used to justify such an exemplary score.

As employers, we could make our lives a whole lot easier if we changed our definitions from "meets/exceeds expectations" to narrative descriptions that better reflect the value behind the numbers. Dick Grote again recommends something along the lines of the following:

Revised Rating Designation	Narrative Description
5. Distinguished Performance	Performance is exemplary by a significant degree.

4. Superior Performance	Performance is continually superior and regularly goes beyond what is expected.
3. Fully Successful	Performance consistently meets the critical requirements of the position; employee performs at the level expected.
2. Needs Improvement	Performance occasionally falls below what is required of the position; individual needs to improve in specified areas.
1. Unsatisfactory	Performance is unacceptable. Immediate and sustained improvement is mandatory. Human Resources will be involved to establish a performance plan.

SOURCE: Dick Grote, *The Performance Appraisal Question and Answer Book* (New York: AMACOM, 2002), p. 166.

Introduce this revised rating system to your company's HR department and see if general management would find benefit in adapting traditional definitions to these enhanced narrative descriptions. You just may find that the old stigma of receiving a 3 on a performance review will give way to a new interpretation that allows your employees to feel proud of that very same numerical grade.

CHAPTER 12

YOU'RE READY TO GO

We've now taken the productive performance appraisal system from beginning to end. As you can see, our recommendations do not include any shortcuts in handing out appraisals. On the contrary, we espouse a system that may very well be more complicated and involve more time (although less work) than you have undertaken in the past. But we strongly believe that you will find the results are worth the effort.

If your job as a supervisor or manager were just to make sure the work got done, you might be able to argue against making the effort to collaborate with your employees in evaluating their job performances and setting goals for the future. But your job should involve more than that. Recognizing that *employees*—not machines, technology, hardware, or money—are your organization's most valuable resources means that you need to work with them to help them do the best work they possibly can. For that, they need your input and guidance. You can give it to them by following the advice mapped out in this book.

Now, let's review the steps you need to follow to successfully conduct productive performance appraisals:

1. *Set goals and identify responsibilities from the onset.* At the time an employee is hired, or whenever a promotion or transfer is given, sit down with the employee and *write down* all the job responsibilities the employee will have. You can also identify areas of weakness (in terms of lack of experience) and set goals for giving employees training and exposure that will allow them to grow in these areas.

2. *Document employee behavior and performance.* Keep a current journal on each of your employees (no matter how small your department may be). Include positive and negative incidents and note any letters of recommendation or disciplinary actions or warnings given to an employee.

3. *Prepare employees to participate in the review process.* Provide your employees with self-evaluation forms well in advance of the appraisal interview. Remind them of what will be discussed during the meeting; ask them to give thought to their future goals and to questions regarding current job concerns.

4. *Prepare yourself for the review process.* Set the interview for a time when you won't be rushed or subject to multiple interruptions. Have ready all necessary and pertinent documentation. Read those documents and refresh your memory before the meeting. Consider future plans for the employee and write them down so that you can present them to the employee at the meeting. Try to anticipate what concerns the employee will want to discuss. Clear your desk and office of distractions. Don't try to "wing it." Set an agenda.

5. *Have an open mind about your employee's future goals.* Allow the employee to make a case for an idea that may not be on your list, and try to help the employee make a plan for how to reach these goals. You may also suggest your own ideas. Remember, this is supposed to be a collaborative process.

6. *Do not discuss compensation until the post-appraisal meeting.* At this point, make sure you have firm commitments from management or human resources regarding any salary increases, training programs, promotions, or transfers that you wish to give the employee. Make no promises that you cannot absolutely deliver.

7. *Follow through on the plans you make with the employee with daily supervision and feedback.* Make the appraisal process a continual one, particularly when you have positive comments to make. Check progress the employee is making toward reaching goals and hold follow-up sessions to rethink strategies if employee progress is not satisfactory.

WHEN WILL I FIND THE TIME?

Does all of this seem overwhelming? It might. We've written down just about everything you need to do to make your employees' performance appraisals valuable and productive. However, now that you've read through the book, you can ask yourself just how much of what we've discussed is already part of your management techniques.

Chances are you're already doing a lot of what we've suggested—at least in part.

For example, you may be documenting only disciplinary problems. It won't be very hard to expand your documentation to include positive performance. Or, you may already be involved in setting job and career goals for your employees. We've now given you a way to incorporate this activity directly into the review process.

We've given you a blueprint for making your employee appraisals productive ones. The execution is up to you. Think about what you want for your employees. More significantly, think about how you'd like to be treated yourself, because that will impact your approach more than anything else. Consider the difference it can make in your department to have employees who are truly committed to improving their job performance and who believe that their manager is committed to helping them do so.

RATING YOURSELF

Are you confident that you now know the difference between a productive performance appraisal and one that does little more than provide a superficial review? Take the following exercise to find out:

EXERCISE: WHAT'S THE DIFFERENCE?

A supervisor might make any of these statements during an appraisal. If you believe the statement is a productive one, check Yes; if not, check No. Compare your answers against the key at the end of the quiz.

1. "I think your best bet is to follow the path that Susan took. She started out just like you, and look how well she's doing now." __ Yes __ No

2. "What do you see as your biggest strength on the job? How do you think you can build on that?" __ Yes __ No

3. "There's no room now for any promotions. You're going to have to find satisfaction in your present job." __ Yes __ No

4. "You're doing everything just fine. I really have no complaints at all. Any problems on your end?" __ Yes __ No

5. "Your performance has been very good. I'm especially pleased with the way you interact with clients. For example, when Mr. Jones was upset last week, you were able to calm him down and minimize any damage to the business relationship." __ Yes __ No

6. "You've really shown tremendous ability in understanding the new technology. Have you given any thoughts to getting more involved in that end of the business?" __ Yes __ No

7. "I can't agree with your assessment that you are diligent about meeting deadlines. I can show you several incidents in this journal when you did not get your work done on time and I had to give you an extension." __ Yes __ No

8. "That's just not a realistic goal. No one I know has ever done it like that before." __ Yes __ No

9. "I can't help but take your poor performance personally. Haven't I given you every chance to do better?" __ Yes __ No

10. "I believe you can do better in meeting quality standards. Why do you think you're having so much trouble in this area?" __ Yes __ No

ANSWERS

1. No. What another individual chose to do can be entirely irrelevant. It is better to give a reason that relates to the employee.

2. Yes. This statement engages the employee and gets her to participate in the evaluation process.

3. No. Approaching the subject in this way accentuates the negative. No one likes to be told what they "have to do."

4. No. This statement pretty much closes off the discussion.

5. Yes. Follow praise with an example of what the employee is doing right. It teaches the employee to keep up the good work and also lets him know that you are aware of what he's doing.

6. Yes. Again, this statement shows you are aware of the employee's talents. It also opens the discussion to a new avenue of opportunity for the employee.

7. Yes. Disagreement is followed up with evidence from the employee journal. That's the way to do it.

8. No. Goal setting should be a collaborative effort. The employee should be free to explore new goals even if the manager does not immediately view it the same way.

9. No. Never take an employee's poor performance personally. This statement sounds more like a parent trying to shame a child than a manager speaking to an employee.

10. Yes. Criticism is given by positively saying the employee can do better. The employee is given a chance to explain herself before the manager makes further criticisms.

A FINAL CHECKLIST

What steps can you take to improve your present appraisal system? Does it need a complete overhaul or will it hold up with some simple adjustments and fine-tuning? To make that assessment, this checklist will give you a head start on how to improve your system. You fill in whatever else is necessary.

❑ Create a system for documenting each of my employee's job performance.

❑ Provide employees with forms to evaluate their own work.

❑ Improve communication with employees so that "performance appraisals" are not dirty words.

❑ Become more familiar with training programs that can help employees grow in their occupations.

❑ Improve my listening and processing skills so that I can better collaborate with my employees on making plans for performance improvement and goal setting.

❑ Practice being more aware of pitfalls in open discussions with my employees. Think before I speak.

Finally, some key lessons from this book are worth repeating one last time:

- A productive appraisal recognizes that people are the most valuable resource of any organization.
- The most important result of the performance appraisal is the actual process itself. Some automatic structure eases this working session, and it can change employee expectations about the performance appraisal.
- Employees should be as prepared for appraisals as you are. It can be quite a revelation just how differently you and your employees perceive their jobs.
- Almost every employee has hopes and aspirations beyond his present job. Proficiency is the key, and positive reinforcement is important.
- "Documentation" is the buzzword. Having the dates and times down on paper can eliminate a lot of denials and accusations.
- Both you and your employee are adults. At the center of the discussion is the employee's livelihood. It's not a time for jokes or idle chat. Take your employee's opinions seriously, but make your choices based on performance and experience, not personality.
- Following precedence is an easy trap to fall into. If you are bound to follow whatever came before you, when do you make the time for improvement?
- It may be hard for some employees to admit they're not performing well. Other people may resent being asked to set new objectives for their job performance. Recognize that you and the employee may have separate agendas.
- When you need an employee to make changes, always have a prepared list and always follow up. Follow-up is essential, especially with a poor performer.
- Sexual harassment has become such a sensitive issue that supervisors need to be extra careful. Watch what you're saying! And avoid the clichés.

■ Money is often a distraction, so keep the discussion of salary out of the appraisal process.

■ Your employees are entitled to see the final rating they have been given.

Armed with these tools, the theory, and the practical application suggestions in this book, you're ready to forge ahead! Don't worry about doing this "perfectly," because human interaction rarely will ever be anything close to perfect. What's important is that you start. Remember as well to keep your staff members' needs ahead of your own: By placing others' needs first, you'll always be respected and admired. Be open and honest when communicating your perception of an individual's performance: People will appreciate your candidness and accept your criticism if it's objective, well supported, and delivered constructively.

Finally, remember that you can tell anyone anything—it's all in your delivery. Show your compassion and demonstrate that you care and your employees will hold themselves to a much higher standard for *your* sake (in addition to theirs). People respect competence, and the performance appraisal process that takes place throughout the year and crystallizes at the time of the annual performance review will demonstrate more than anything else your competence in leading and guiding others for their own (career) good and for the good of the company. That's *selfless leadership*, so keep studying the guidelines in this book to strengthen that "portable" skill that will help you stand out as a rarity among your peers throughout your own career.

And therein lies the beauty of the whole system: The return on investment for this workplace activity, more so than any other, reflects *your* potential for growth and ability to lead through others. Put others' needs first, elevate those who look to you for guidance, and watch how your own job satisfaction and career opportunities multiply. What a great way to spend a career and create an environment where others can motivate themselves and thank you for being their mentor. Good luck!

INDEX

adults, treating employees as,
58–60
appearance, commenting on, 87
appraisal interview, 15–16
checklist, 30
assignments, adding new, 17
attitude
paternalistic, 58–60
patronizing, 55
problems of, 83–84
avoidance by employee, response
to, 85

bad news, 78–86
bias, journal and claim of, 47
boss, *see* supervisor

career development, supervisor
help with, 34–38
career objectives, 33
employee preparation for discussion, 65
and planning, 39
change
exploring need for, 65–66
specificity in describing need, 80
clamming up, response to, 85
clichés, 27–30, 59
comments, on appearance, 87
commitment
renewal by plateaued employee,
41
to training, 81

communication
discussing skills, 21–22
in performance review, 55
comparison of employee with others, 56
compensation discussion, 16, 17,
56, 90
time for, 100–101
conduct infractions, 83
confrontation, problems from
avoiding, 48
conversation, 6
counseling, for plateaued employee, 39, 41–42
court proceedings, performance
appraisal weight in, 58
"critical incidence diaries," 44
crying, response to, 85

differentiation, in performance appraisal, 48
documentation, 105
to avoid negative surprises,
49–50
employee journal, 43
employee journal contents,
45–46
for objectivity, 50–53
of poor performance, 80
as protection, 46–49
reasons for, 43–45

emotional outbursts, dealing with,
84–85
employee
adjusting expectations of, 38
agreement on performance improvement, 82
asking for input from, 7, 26–27
comparison with others, 56
counseling for plateaued, 39,
41–42
discussion of others, 89
goals for, 65–66
long-term and short-term goals,
33, 81
perception of job, vs. supervisor,
11
preparing for appraisal, 62–66,
105
relationship with boss, 7–8
resentment, 72–73
response to opinion, 73
treating as adult, 58–60
employee development, 33
employee journal
appropriate contents, 52–53
and bias claim, 47
maintaining for employee, 43
starting, 45–46
errors, avoiding in performance review, 55
expectations, adjusting employee's,
38

"fairness test," 47, 48–49
family, hazard of discussing, 88
feedback, from managers, fre-
quency, 100–101
feelings, do you or don't you testing, 8–9
focus, on interest areas, 38
follow-up after appraisal of poor
performer, 85–86

goals, 105
clash on, 73–76

dos and don'ts guide on choices,
76
for employee, 65–66
input from employee, 7
preparing, 6
questions about, 76–77
short-term and long-term, 33, 81
gossip, 89
Grote, Dick, 101, 102

"halo and horns" effect, 56
honesty, about future options for
poor performer, 81–82
hostility, response to, 85
human assets, return on investment, viii

incident reports, in employee journal, 45
inconsistency, risk of, 56–57
information, in performance review, 55
input from employee, asking for, 7,
26–27
interim reviews, 98
interview for appraisal, 15–16, 30
beginning, 18–21
questions about goals, 76–77

job analysis form, 11–13, 62–63
in time line, 97
use in meeting, 19, 54
job description, 11–12
disagreement on, 70–72
in employee journal, 45
gaining agreement on, 72–73
job objectives worksheet, sample,
40
job responsibilities, misimpercep-
tions on, 69–77
journal
appropriate contents, 52–53
and bias claim, 47
maintaining for employee, 43
reviewing, 57
starting, 45–46

language, 59
layoffs, decisions on, 47–48
leadership, selfless, 110
legal proceedings, performance appraisal weight in, 58
long-term goals of employee, 33

meeting
post-appraisal, 16–17, 95–103
see also interview for appraisal
memo to staff about changes, 64–65
in time line, 97
mentor, plateaued employee as, 41
merit pool, 102
misinformation, 56
misperceptions, on job responsibilities, 69–77
money discussion, 16, 17, 56, 90
time for, 100–101

"negative surprises," avoiding, 49–50
negativity, in performance review, 55
neutral topics, dangers of, 88

objectives, career, 33
objectivity, documentation for, 50–53
office politics, 89
open-mindedness, to employee goals, 105
opinions, performance journal and, 53

participation of employee, 62
paternalistic attitude, 58–60
patronizing attitude, 55
pay discussion, 16, 17, 56, 90
time for, 100–101
perception of job
employee vs. supervisor, 11
sharing differences, 15

performance appraisals
checklist for improving, 108
guidelines for poor performer, 80–83
misperceptions, 3–4
preparation checklist, 60–61
summary of process, 97–99
supervisors' impression of, vii
weight in court proceedings, 58
written warning as part, 82
see also bad news
performance journal
appropriate contents, 52–53
and bias claim, 47
maintaining for employee, 43
starting, 45–46
"performance logs," 44
performance ratings
revised system, 102–103
spread of scores, 101–102
performance review, avoiding errors, 55
performance traits discussion, vs. superficial compliments, 15
performance/work habits review, 11, 13–14, 23–28
sample, 24
in time line, 97
pitfalls, 87–92
plan, developing, 38–39
plateaued employee, counseling for, 39, 41–42
politics, as topic to avoid, 88
poor performer
follow-up after appraisal, 85–86
guidelines for, 80–83
positive reinforcement, 41
post-appraisal meeting, 16–17, 95–103
precedence, 70
preparation for appraisal, 10–11
employee's, 62–66
supervisor's, 54–61
problem areas, discussion of, 25–26

process, 6–8
productive appraisals, 5–6
  benefits, 5
progress reports, in employee journal, 45, 46
promises, 17, 89–90
promotion, 17
protection, documentation as,
  46–49
"psychic" income, 7
purpose of appraisal, misperceptions, 5

quality of performance, discussing,
  21–26
quality standards, written, 80
questions, asking about goals,
  76–77

ratings for performance
  revised system, 102–103
  spread of scores, 101–102
"recency effect," 44
religion, as topic to avoid, 88
resentment by employee, 72–73
responsibilities of supervisor, 99
responsibility, for reaching goals,
  39
return on investment, of human
  assets, viii
rights of supervisor, 99
roles, disagreement on, 69

salary discussion, 16, 17, 56, 90
  time for, 100–101, 105
secret weapon, 7
self-assessment, 14
  reviewing, 55
  vs. supervisor review, 23–24
selfless leadership, 110
sexual harassment, 87–88
short-term goals of employee, 33

shouting, response to, 85
status quo, 99–100
suggestions, for performance improvement, 21
supervisor
  career development help from,
    34–38
  employee relationship with, 7–8
  perception of job, vs. employee,
    11
  preparation for appraisal by,
    54–61
  rights and responsibilities of, 99
  self-rating, 106–108
surprises, avoiding negative, 49–50

testing feelings, do you or don't
  you, 8–9
time, requirements for appraisals,
  106
time limits, setting for performance
  improvement, 82
time line for performance appraisal, 97–99
timing
  for reporting incidents, 44
  for salary discussion, 100–101
titles, 69–70
trainer, plateaued employee as, 41
training
  committing to, 81
  value of, 38
trends, in performance review, 57

unsatisfactory performance rating,
  79

weaknesses, discussion of, 25–26
"winging it," problems from, 56
"work habits," 23
written warning, 58
  in substandard performance re-
    view, 82

ABOUT THE AUTHORS

Paul Falcone is a human resources executive and the author of many best-selling books, including *2600 Phrases for Effective Performance Reviews, The Hiring and Firing Question and Answer Book, 101 Sample Write-Ups for Documenting Employee Performance Problems,* and *96 Great Interview Questions to Ask Before You Hire* (all published by AMACOM). He is a regular contributor to *HR Magazine* and an instructor in the UCLA Extension School of Business and Management. He holds bachelor's and master's degrees from UCLA and lives in Valencia, California.

Randi Sachs is a freelance business writer. She lives in Merrick, New York.

Announcing!